SpringerBriefs in Law

More information about this series at http://www.springer.com/series/10164

Federico Ferretti

EU Competition Law, the Consumer Interest and Data Protection

The Exchange of Consumer Information in the Retail Financial Sector

 Springer

Federico Ferretti
Brunel Law School
Brunel University London
Uxbridge
Middlesex
UK

ISSN 2192-855X   ISSN 2192-8568   (electronic)
ISBN 978-3-319-08905-8   ISBN 978-3-319-08906-5   (eBook)
DOI 10.1007/978-3-319-08906-5

Library of Congress Control Number: 2014944337

Springer Cham Heidelberg New York Dordrecht London

Printed on acid-free paper

Springer is part of Springer Science+Business Media (www.springer.com)

To Stella, Giacomo, and Oliver—with love,
too much love

Foreword

Information has always been critical to the functioning of a market economy. It enables innovation and is a primary driver of resource allocation and price discovery in markets. But, information plays a particularly important role in financial services. Indeed, financial products are not physical, material goods but constructed from packages of information bound together by legal contracts.

If used properly, information can lead to competitive, well-functioning, responsive markets that meet the needs of citizen-consumers more fairly and efficiently. But, if information is not used within a proper framework, it can result in dysfunctional markets, market abuse, major consumer detriment including social and financial exclusion, discrimination and, in some cases, abuse of fundamental rights.

Therefore, the fundamental issue for policymakers and lawmakers is: do greater information flows and exchange improve overall citizen-consumer welfare? To answer this question, we need a proper framework to judge the positive and negative aspects of information flows and exchange.

There has been a significant amount of analysis and study undertaken on the role of information in market economies and within specific markets. But looking at the literature we can see that this has focused primarily on issues such as risk management, information flows and price discovery and addressing information asymmetries to promote competition, more efficient market and improve consumer protection. The assumption behind these theoretical models seems to be that (a) increased information flows and exchange will lead to more efficient competition in markets which in turn will result in better outcomes for consumers and (b) recognising that markets can produce negative outcomes, information disclosure allows citizen-consumers to protect themselves from adverse market practices and behaviours. The assumption seems to be that even with the risks involved, greater information flows and exchange produce a net benefit for citizen-consumers.

Even the basic assumption that information flows and exchange lead to more effective competition, which in turn results in improved outcomes, needs to be challenged. To be sure, competition and innovation have delivered real benefits.

But the experience of consumer advocates has been that aggressive competition, far from improving consumer welfare, has often resulted in serious detriment and welfare loss. There is a very real difference between aggressive competitive activity and competition that works in the citizen-consumer interest, and spurious innovations and truly socially useful innovation.

So even on their own narrow terms, these economic models are very limited. However, there is an even more fundamental problem with these models and gaps in the academic literature.

In this dominant market paradigm, the role of citizen-consumers is relegated to one of economic actors in the pursuit of the ultimate goal of economic efficiency. The dominant models focus on the economic interests of citizen-consumers but do not give anywhere near sufficient consideration to the social dimension or the fundamental rights of citizen-consumers including their basic information rights. These limited market models do not allow policymakers and lawmakers to assess the extent to which the pursuit of economic goals conflicts with social justice goals or the pursuit of fundamental citizens' rights. Indeed, it could be argued that, as a result, the policymaking and decision-making process at the heart of political, economic and social life is intrinsically flawed.

As mentioned, information exchange has always been at the core of market activity but the need to reformulate our thinking on the role of information in markets is even more critical given the rapid developments in information science, technological innovation and the sheer volume of data and information in financial markets (the so-called 'Big Data' issue).

With this in mind, I am very pleased to provide the Foreword for this important book which looks at the issue of information in EU financial markets—in particular information exchanges between competitors under EU competition law. This is a very important contribution to thinking on this critical issue.

Mick McAteer

Chairman—Financial Services Users Group (European Commission)
Non-Executive Board Member—Financial Conduct Authority (UK)
Founder and Director of the Financial Inclusion Centre (UK)

Contents

Abbreviations

CCD	Consumer Credit Directive 2008/48/EC
Charter	Charter of Fundamental Rights of the European Union
CJEU	Court of Justice of the European Union (previously, European Court of Justice)
EU	European Union
MCD	Mortgage Credit Directive 2014/17/EU
SMEs	Small and Medium Enterprises
TEC	Treaty on European Communities
TEU	Treaty on European Union
TFEU	Treaty on the Functioning of the European Union

Chapter 1
Introduction

This work revisits the issue of the legitimacy or illegitimacy of information exchanges among competitors under EU competition law. This is not a new topic but nevertheless it remains a challenging one since the Court of Justice of the European Union (CJEU), the European Commission, and academic scholarship have not provided defined general or theoretical rules but they have offered guiding principles to be used on a case-by-case basis.

Against this background, the focus of this work is the consumer financial market in the European Union (EU). It re-examines the exchange of consumer financial data among competing financial institutions from the perspective of European competition law, market integration, and the interest of consumers vis-à-vis the peculiarities of the sector and the potential detriment that it may pose to consumers. The aim is to provide a critical analysis and assess to what extent the case-law and official guidance offered by the competent European competition authorities have provided clarity in the sector and at the same time have offered solutions that are suitable for competition purposes, foster market integration, but that ultimately work for consumers. Financial services generally, and consumer finance in particular, are a key and sensitive sector of the economy. The large majority of households and small businesses have dealings with providers of financial services and access to such services is increasingly considered as a necessary condition for participation in the economy and society generally.

Moreover, since consumer information is involved, this book analyses to what extent the protection of personal data interacts with competition law and the interest of consumers. Data protection is a personality right of individuals, elevated to a fundamental right of the EU to safeguard the dignity of the members of its society. It is a legal right which aims to protect fundamental values of the European society, which may interfere with the economic sphere and business interests. Among these values, for example, data protection aims at preventing the conforming of economic

© The Author(s) 2014

F. Ferretti, *EU Competition Law, the Consumer Interest and Data Protection*,
SpringerBriefs in Law, DOI 10.1007/978-3-319-08906-5_1

and social behaviours, standardisations, classifications, categorisations, sorting, exclusion, and discrimination of individuals.

Hence, the juxtaposition of fundamental rights with economic objectives may not always lead in the same direction and the judiciary may be faced with conflicting interests in the enforcement of the law.

What the sophistication of financial markets and their close link with the lives of individuals have shown these years is that the protection of the individual consumer is a fundamental part of maintaining human dignity and a necessary precondition for his/her full participation in the economic, social, and democratic life of society.

Thus, the subject of the exchange of consumer financial information is special because if on the one hand it presents jurists with the usual difficulties inherent of this area of competition law, on the other hand it has a strong impact on consumer protection policy as well as on the interference of markets with fundamental rights. Likewise, retail finance is a well-known area where much work is still needed to achieve the internal market.[1]

So far, the debate has centred on the traditional view that information exchange is a common feature of competitive markets and it is either capable of generating efficiency gains or it may lead to restrictions of competition especially where undertakings become aware of market strategies of their competitors. The determination between the two depends on the features of the market in which the exchange takes place and the type of information exchanged.[2] Likewise, until now the assessment of the consumer interest in the context of competition has mostly focused on market efficiency assuming that this maximises automatically economic gains for consumers, hence their welfare.[3]

Yet, an established aim of EU competition policy is the achievement of the objectives of the European treaties, which include the achievement of the internal market, the approximation of economic policies, the promotion of growth and the raising of living standards, etc. in a space where consumers receive an adequate protection.[4] All this should be achieved under a framework which aims at the protection of the fundamental rights of the members of society within the EU.[5]

In this context, new literature has started putting forward the concept that in tandem competition law and consumer law can and should guarantee adequate protection for consumers, not only safeguarding their immediate material prosperity but also raising their quality of life and redressing unfair situations in the

---

[1] See, for example, European Central Bank (2009).

[2] See, generally, Capobianco (2004), pp. 1247–1276; Bergman (2006), pp. 11–17; Teece (1994), pp. 465–481, Niemeyer (1993), pp. 151–156. A latest account is in Lorenz (2013).

[3] See, generally, Buttigieg (2009), Whish (2012), Van den Bergh and Camesasca (2006).

[4] For e.g. see Article 12 TEU (ex Article 153(2) TEC) which states that "consumer protection requirements shall be taken into account in defining and implementing other Union policies and activities". See also Article 38 of the Charter of Fundamental Rights of the EU which states that "Union policies shall ensure a high level of consumer protection".

[5] See generally the Charter of the Fundamental Rights of the EU.

market.[6] Markets may work efficiently but not fairly, so competition and consumer law cannot work separately.

Embracing this idea, this study moves a step forward adding to the equation the safeguard of fundamental rights as part of the consumer interest, where in truth it is the interest of society generally that reflects on the interest of consumers. Arguably, competition law cannot be oblivious of the type of society where Europeans aim to live in.

The peculiarity of the exchange of consumer financial data by financial entities offers such an opportunity, to show how competition law cannot be assessed in the abstract and in isolation as it has been done so far by the competent European competition authorities. On the contrary, the suggestion is that a holistic approach encompassing consumer protection and fundamental rights is the desirable way forward.

Above all, this work aims to take the perspective of the protection of the fundamental rights and freedoms of individuals in their social and economic context. This stance does not deny the relevance of economic analysis but it is equally concerned with the subsistence and preservation of other values which are equally, if not primarily, in the interest of consumers. Indeed, far from challenging the economic theory about the importance of information in financial markets or the economic goals of competition policy and law, the basic problem of this work is to gauge how, and to what extent, the application of such general economic theories as applied by decision makers could be influenced when consumers are involved, having consideration not only of broader social concerns but also of their rights as recognised in the EU.

Likewise, this study does not disrespect *per se* the economic interests of the financial services industry. Indeed, it does not intend to endorse any anti-capitalist message, and considers profitability a perfectly legitimate interest to be carried out and ideally achieved. But the basic premise taken is that to disregard the social dimension of consumers, their protection, and the legal protection afforded to rights in pursuit of economic efficiency is of concern and impermissible. Competition law enforcement should be no exception and it should not delegate these matters to other areas of law or dismiss their consideration on the basis of other regulatory failures at other levels of policy and law-making. Otherwise, the integrity of the legal system as a whole would be put in jeopardy and at risk.

To address the questions or the arguments that it aims to advance, Chap. 2 analyses the economic rationales and objectives of exchanging consumer information among competitors in retail financial markets, showing the vast range of economic theories justifying the practice. The organisational settings are explored, alongside relevant policy objectives that inform the legal form or institutional arrangements within the EU. The partition between the different purposes and institutional arrangements that justify the exchange of information among competing financial institutions is important to set the scene for the purpose of

---

[6] Buttigieg (2009), sp. 1–3.

competition law and to qualify the information exchanges among competing financial institutions, establishing which other areas beyond competition goals are affected and need attention.

Chapter 3 revisits the traditional approach taken on the controversial issue of information exchanges among competitors under EU competition law generally. It provides an overview of the case-law and the scholarly debate to establish the legal framework and guidance provided. The aim is to show the continuing difficulty of establishing a clear framework despite the intervention of the competent authorities and academic analysis. Thus, the debate is transferred to the retail financial sector and its landmark case *Asnef Equifax v. Ausbanc (Asnef)*.[7] The aim is to show how the CJEU has applied and interpreted competition law in the retail financial sector and the conclusions that it has reached, informing *inter alia* the European Commission in drafting its 'Guidelines on the applicability of Article 101 of the Treaty on the Functioning of the European Union to horizontal co-operation agreements' *(2011Guidelines)*.[8] A specification of the type of information addressed by the European competition authorities and a critique as to the economic and legal assumptions that they take reveal an ongoing uncertainty and unsatisfactory state in the sector.

Chapter 4 analyses the exchange of information in the context of the integration of the EU retail financial market. This is also where it addresses the case law and guidelines of the competition authorities to show the shortcomings of the current state of affairs. Whilst the latter have provided answers to the pro-competitive market entry of foreign lenders in the national markets of the Member States, all other aspects of European integration have been underestimated or neglected, contributing to the segmentation of the retail finance markets into national ones. This part of the book also investigates how the oversight of the information market in the competition analysis risks frustrating the legislative efforts put forward by the EU in the area of financial market integration and credit for consumers. Similarly, it examines how the failure to consider the information market as a relevant market may lead to unexplored competition concerns. The final part of the chapter, in fact, analyses to what extent the assessment of the horizontal competition among financial institutions may neglect the role of information providers and their vertical integration, as well as possible forms of national monopolies and concentrations.

Finally, Chap. 5 focuses on the legal framework emerging from the CJEU decision and the *2011Guidelines*. This is the objective of the criticisms from the angle first above stated in this work. It investigates who is the consumer considered by the competition authorities and it compares them with the image of the consumer under consumer law. Next, it looks at the consequences of taking a diverging concept of who is the consumer, what their interest is, and what are the

---

[7] *Asnef-Equifax, Servicios de Información sobre Solvencia y Crédito, SL v Asociación de Usuarios de Servicios Bancarios (Ausbanc)* (Case C-238/05), [2006] ECR I-11125.

[8] In OJ 2011, C 1/25.

detriments for consumers and their economic and social inclusion. In addition, in this chapter the fundamental right of data protection is brought into the equation in the assessment of the consumer interest. The fundamental question as to the integrity of the legal system as a whole is addressed and analysed. Likewise, it is explored the argument of the desirability of avoiding the assessment of competition law as a legal discipline separate from other areas of policy and law. Finally, the last part of the chapter touches upon the unexplored territory of the relationship between data protection and competition law.

Ultimately, all chapters together, this study aims to show that the current position of the CJEU and the guiding principles of the European Commission are unsuitable or at least questionable on many accounts, arguably for the myopia of applying competition law in isolation as a legal box on its own.

References

Bergman M (2006) Introduction. In: Swedish Competition Authority (ed) The pros and cons of information sharing. Leanders Grafiska, Stockholm, pp 11–17

Buttigieg E (2009) Competition law: safeguarding the consumer interest. Kluwer, The Netherlands

Capobianco A (2004) Information exchange under EC competition law. Common Mark Law Rev 41:1247–1276

European Central Bank (2009) Financial integration in Europe. Frankfurt

Lorenz M (2013) An introduction to EU competition law. Cambridge University Press, Cambridge

Niemeyer HJ (1993) Market information systems. Eur Compet Law Rev 14:151–156

Teece DJ (1994) Information sharing, innovation and antitrust. Antitrust Law J 62:465–481

Van den Bergh RJ, Camesasca PD (2006) European competition law and economics: a comparative perspective. Thomson Sweet and Maxwell, London

Whish R (2012) Competition law. Oxford University Press, Oxford

Chapter 2
Information Exchanges Among Competitors in EU Retail Financial Markets

In principle, each commercial venture is supposed to develop its own experience and knowledge of the market, which become a competitive asset to be used in its business strategies, offers, pricing, and marketing. Without a doubt, market intelligence is a key element of the competitiveness of commercial entities.

Nevertheless, it is now a common feature in the retail financial sector that competitors exchange information about their customers, hence their knowledge and experience. This has become the most extensively used instrument or practice of the credit industry to underwrite decisions on borrowings or the supply of goods and/or services to consumer customers. Lenders, in fact, access credit reference databases and other information managed by third party providers in order to evaluate a consumer's credit application, the risks involved in the financing, and the prospective borrower's creditworthiness.

The rapid development and sophistication of information technologies and systems, coupled with the increasing competition between lenders and issues of borrowers' indebtedness, have made information sharing mechanisms in the credit market a topic of increasing interest among policy makers and academics in a number of disciplines. In particular, economists have long stressed the importance of information in credit markets. They support the development and expansion of data sharing in the financial system in order to meet the problem of asymmetrical information between borrowers and lenders, as well as problems of bad selection of customers, and the risk which arises from the characteristics of prospective borrowers that may increases the possibility of an economic loss.

In addition, new trends in the use of consumer financial information are beginning to emerge that make some justification for the expanding use of these data.

Thus, it is important to examine how and why competing financial institutions in the retail finance sector exchange information about their customers, as well as the third-party actors involved in the centralisation and subsequent dissemination

© The Author(s) 2014
F. Ferretti, *EU Competition Law, the Consumer Interest and Data Protection*,
SpringerBriefs in Law, DOI 10.1007/978-3-319-08906-5_2

of such information. In particular, the needs or problems that such exchanges aim to address or fix, and the functions in the economy that they purport to reach, become important in the understanding of the sector. The interests or rights at stake in an information exchange are a central theme in the rationale of any economic activity and legal framework of economic activities, especially if conflicting ones emerge or if they pose concerns for existing areas of law such as competition law enforcement. Different actors involved in a business process, in fact, may have different interests and, at times, they may attract rights. To the extent that these are or may be diverging, the determination of the prevailing interests to be protected or the balance to be struck, as the case may be, constitute a precondition of a legal analysis aiming at assessing the legitimacy of the system, or whether the law provides satisfactory answers or not.

2.1 Classical Economic Theory and Competition

2.1.1 Information Asymmetries, Adverse Selection, and Creditworthiness

Information asymmetry makes reference to the different knowledge or information that one party of a commercial transaction has over the other party. Economists have identified the problem of asymmetrical information as the one that a party has when it does not have the same information of the other party in relation to the risks relating to the performance of the contract by such other party. In basic terms, one party knows less than the other, a situation which is different from the one where a party has less information than the ideal, known as 'imperfect information'.

In retail finance, this may be seen as the different knowledge or level of information that customers have either on financial products or the market behaviour of providers. Similarly, from the perspective of suppliers within the same relationship, this difference of knowledge or information relates to the payment behaviour of customers. In a credit relationship, lenders want to avoid lending money that will not be repaid. If they do not have the same information as borrowers have on their ability or willingness to repay a debt, they will incur in a higher risk of making bad business. This risk poses problems of bad debts and adverse selection, i.e. the selection of the wrong customers.[1]

Hence, economic theory has long stressed the importance of information in credit markets.

From the supply side, the reduction of asymmetric information and adverse selection of customers encompass several elements relating to market structure and marketing activities of the participants in the retail finance marketplace.

---

[1] Stiglitz and Weiss (1981), pp. 393–410; Berger and Udell (1995), pp. 351–381.

In summarised terms, the theory suggests that the lack of information on borrowers can prevent the efficient allocation of credit in a market and that one way that lenders can improve their knowledge of borrowers is through their observation of clients over time.[2]

In turn, the reduction of asymmetric information affects many aspects of the lending business: risk management and pricing through the assessment of uncertainties about the ability and/or willingness of a debtor to repay, market entry and competition, customers' creditworthiness, application processing and screening, customers' segmentation and product specialisation, and improvement of the credit portfolio.[3]

Typically, the process of granting credit begins when a prospective customer approaches a credit provider and applies for credit or services/goods to be paid at a later stage. In the event the latter agrees to enter the financing or credit agreement, then, such a relationship ends when the last statement of the credit line is paid back in accordance with the same agreement or, in the worst case scenario, when the credit is unrecoverable and/or disregarded following a debt recovery proceeding and a judicial procedure, or in some jurisdictions the judicial declaration of insolvency of the borrower. The recourse to debt collection procedures and legal actions, however, does not guarantee to lenders the recovery of the debt and, in any event, they are considered an instrument of last resort as they are perceived to be both costly and time-consuming.[4]

Thus, risk assessment and applicants screening have become particularly important for the consumer credit industry which has to deal with a large number of small-sum (often unsecured) credit lines. It is widely agreed, in fact, that in this sector profitability is only achieved by minimising the risk while ensuring that a sizeable volume of credit lines is granted. Hence, credit grantors consider information about borrowers vital for their risk-assessment purposes. Along these lines, one of the best predictors of future behaviour is considered to be past behaviour. Therefore, information on how a potential borrower has met obligations in the past enables lenders to more accurately evaluate credit risk, easing adverse selection problems.[5]

Moreover, the small or medium size of loans to consumers means that it is not cost-efficient to assess consumers on a case by case basis. Traditionally, when lenders evaluate borrowers to determine their creditworthiness for credit-risk assessment and management, they interview the applicants and ask them directly for personal information together with the relevant supporting documents. At the same time, they seek and gather information from their own databases developed through years of experience and business practice in the credit market. Such a

---

[2] Ibid.

[3] Stiglitz and Weiss (1981), pp. 393–410; Akelof (1970), pp. 523–547; Berger and Udell (1995), pp. 351–381; Diamond (1991), pp. 689–721; Admati and Pfleiderer (2000), pp. 479–519.

[4] Riestra (2002), 4; Bertola et al. (2006a), pp. 347–371.

[5] Miller (2003a), pp. 1–23, sp. 2. See also Miller (2003b), 25–79.

source of information, however, is incomplete as it covers a lender's own past and present customers, but it does not contain data about the same customers' past and/or present relationship with other financial institutions nor, from a competition perspective, information about new or prospective customers and their past and/or present relationship with other providers. Thus, it is with the view to supplement comprehensive information about these customers that information exchanges among competitors and sophisticated centralised databases emerged and developed in the past few decades.[6]

2.1.2 Competition

As far as competition is concerned, the exchange of information on customer relationships or applicants reduces the information monopoly of individual lenders and the competitive advantage of large financial institutions. Although lenders lose the exclusivity of data in terms of competition one versus the other, they would ultimately gain by sharing information as this additional accumulation of data enables them to distinguish the good borrowers from the bad ones. Information sharing would serve as a tool to predict the future payment behaviour of applicants allowing lenders to attract creditworthy borrowers and offering them better terms and conditions, thus promoting market competition that could ultimately result in benefits to those 'good consumers'.[7] Hence, the adverse selection problem identified by the economic literature indicates that should lenders fail to distinguish the good borrowers from the bad ones, all accepted borrowers would be charged at a higher rate an average interest rate that mirrors their pooled experience.[8] Therefore, the distinction between good borrowers from the bad ones allows lenders on the one hand to offer more advantageous prices to lower-risk borrowers while, on the other hand, higher risk borrowers are offered higher interest rates or can be rationed out of the market because of the lenders' unwillingness to offer these borrowers accommodating rates or any credit at all.[9]

The problem of asymmetric information and adverse selection becomes greater for new market entrants, particularly foreign lenders. This is particularly the case in the context of the creation of the EU single market and cross-border entry or cross-border provision of financial services. In addition to competitive disadvantages in relation to incurring greater risks of incorrectly estimating a borrower's credit risk, without relevant information on borrowers new market entrants would be likely to attract precisely those who were rejected by existing lenders in the market.[10] This

---

[6] Bertola et al. (2006b), pp. 347–371; Riestra (2002).

[7] European Commission (2009).

[8] Alary and Gollier (2001).

[9] Barron and Staten (2000, 2003), pp. 273–310.

[10] Giannetti et al. (2010).

circumstances has induced recent literature to conclude that information sharing, market structure, and competitive conduct are intrinsically intertwined in the financial services market and, from the standpoint of industrial organisation, the availability of information shared by the sector can affect foreign lenders' choice not only of whether to entry another jurisdiction but also the mode of doing it, i.e. whether through the cross-border provision of services, the setting up of branches or subsidiaries or through mergers and acquisitions.[11]

Therefore, on the one hand such strategies may well have the potential to influence the intensity of competition in national markets and among national providers. On the other hand, however, this is an indication that the behaviour of one or few market players—particularly existing lenders—influences and drives the behaviour of others, especially new entrants, which will decide their strategies on the experience, or market intelligence, of existing ones.

Prima facie, considerations of the like may have the effect of casting doubts as to whether or to what extent in actual facts this may constitute a concerted practice or simply a reduction of market uncertainty, which will be discussed further below.

Also, to the extent that information monopoly of individual lenders is reduced, the information monopoly is transferred to those third-party subjects which become the providers of information and manage the corresponding databases.

This, in turn, may raise new concerns over market competition and power further discussed later in this work.

Yet, there are further justifications to exchange consumer financial information among competing firms.

2.2 Moral Hazard and Reputation Collateral

All financial transactions in general, and credit transactions in particular, involve risks or uncertainties. Among these, a dominant one concerns the ability and/or the willingness to repay of the debtor, known as 'transactional risks'. At the time of contracting, lenders want to assess whether borrowers will have the ability to pay when the repayment is due back and/or that they have the willingness to pay back their debt. These are two different types of risk because some people may be able to pay but unwilling to do it, or vice versa, they do want to pay but due to unexpected changes in their circumstances they may be unable to pay back when the money is due.

The unwillingness to repay is known as 'moral hazard'. It refers to the risk which arises from personal, as distinguished from physical, characteristics of a borrower that increases the possibility of an economic loss. It is a phenomenon normally associated with business credit (also referred as 'producer credit'): it occurs when entrepreneurs have incentives to invest in riskier projects and a larger

---

[11] Ibid.

proportion of the cost is financed by a lender. If the project is successful, they have much to gain from any excess return, but if the project fails their losses would be limited by bankruptcy. Hence, in this circumstance, as lenders will suffer much of the actual economic losses, borrowers do not have incentives to act prudently and exceed in risk-taking to attempt to maximise returns. Investments, then, are deemed to become capable of being safer if entrepreneurs have more to lose, in particular if they are forced to bear a portion of the risk.[12]

But moral hazard is now considered directly relevant also for the behaviour of consumers in the use of consumptive credit every time that a repayment reflects the willingness, not the ability, to honour one's debts. As the theory explains, when deciding to repay, a rational agent weighs the gain of failing to repay vis-à-vis the punishment for default. Since small-size debts could not be cost-effective to recover by lenders, and debtors may receive no or little punishment by the law (it may take the form of personal bankruptcy in the few jurisdictions where it exist), a number of consumers may become prone to moral-hazard, i.e. they willingly may decide not to repay their debts.[13]

Similarly, economic theory also explains that information exchanges among lenders play a pivotal role as a borrowers' discipline device as the latter would know that a delay or a default in re-payment compromise their reputation with all the other potential lenders on the market, resulting in credit with more costly terms or by cutting them off from credit entirely.[14] Therefore, information exchanges among lenders would strengthen borrower discipline and reduce moral hazard, since late payment or failure to repay a debt with one institution would result in sanctions by all or many others. According to Miller, a borrower's 'good name', i.e. his or her reputation collateral, should provide "an incentive to meet commitments much the same way as does a pledge of physical collateral, thus reducing moral hazard".[15]

From this perspective, some have controversially gone as far as suggesting that information exchanges maintain accountability and honesty in society.[16]

2.3 Responsible Lending

The market for loans available to consumers, be it consumer or mortgage credit, has grown rapidly in the last decade across the EU and it is becoming increasingly sophisticated. However, with the development of the retail and mortgage credit markets European consumers are becoming increasingly indebted. The growth of

---

[12] Bertola et al. (2006a), pp. 1–26.

[13] Ibid.

[14] Jappelli and Pagano (2002), pp. 2017–2045; Diamond (1991), pp. 689–721; Admati and Pfleiderer (2000), pp. 479–519. See also Jappelli and Pagano (2006), pp. 347–371.

[15] Miller (2003a), pp. 1–23, sp. 2. See also Miller (2003b), pp. 25–79.

[16] Klein (1992), pp. 117–136; Klein (1997), pp. 267–288.

the over-indebtedness of consumers is becoming a concern for national and EU policy-makers alike. Besides, the on-going global credit and financial crisis has raised important issues regarding the protection of consumers in financial markets and the need for additional safeguards to stem the social problems that the crisis has exacerbated.[17]

Therefore, alongside the advancement of measures for the cross-border provision of credit and the abolition of obstacles for further integration, the promotion of responsible lending and borrowing policies to limit the over-indebtedness of European consumers are high on the EU agenda. Likewise, the importance of the relationship between borrowers and financial institutions is under the close scrutiny of European policy makers.

Responsible lending and borrowing is a recent policy introducing a novel concept to tackle consumers' over-indebtedness. It makes reference to the delivery of responsible and reliable markets, as well as the restoration of consumer confidence, where credit products are appropriate for consumers' needs and are tailored to their ability to repay their debts. They envisage a framework that could ensure that all lenders and intermediaries act in a fair, honest and professional manner before, during, and after the lending transaction. Similarly, it is expected that in order to obtain credit consumers provide relevant, complete and accurate information on their finances. They are also encouraged to make informed and sustainable borrowing decisions.[18]

The resulting EU law regarding loans to consumers comprises the Consumer Credit Directive (CCD)[19] and the Mortgage Credit Directive (MCD).[20]

---

[17] See European Commission, *Staff Working Paper on National Measures and Practices aimed at Avoiding Foreclosure Procedures for Residential Mortgage Loans* SEC(2011) 357 final, which pointed to the severe consequences for individual homeowners losing their homes in a foreclosure procedure, but also for society as a whole, considering their impact on financial and social stability.

[18] See Communication of the European Commission to the European Council of 4 March 2009 *Driving European Recovery*, COM (2009) 114. See also the *Public Consultation on Responsible Lending and Borrowing*, available atec.europa.eu/internal…/responsible_lending/consultation_en.pdf. the EU Commission has recently conducted a consultation with all stakeholders on responsible lending and borrowing in the EU to find measures to adequately assess, by all appropriate means, borrowers' creditworthiness before granting them a loan and tackle over-indebtedness. The consultation covered, among other things, the advertising and marketing of credit products, the information to be provided to borrowers prior to granting any loans, ways to assess product suitability and borrower creditworthiness, advice standards, responsible borrowing and issues relating to the framework for credit intermediaries (for example, disclosures, registration, licensing and supervision).

[19] Directive 2008/48/EC of the European Parliament and of the Council of 23 April 2008 on credit agreements for consumers and repealing Council Directive 87/102/EEC, OJ 2008 L 133/66.

[20] Directive 2014/17/EU of the European Parliament and of the Council of 4 February 2014 on credit agreements for consumers relating to residential immovable property and amending Directives 2008/48/EC and 2013/36/EU and Regulation (EU) No 1093/2010, OJ 2014 L 60/34.

The relevant provisions are contained in Articles 8 and 9 of the CCD and Articles 18, 20, and 21 of the MCD.

The CCD is not explicit and it is to some extent unclear on the exchange of consumer information, at least as far as the obligation to share information is concerned. Article 8 of the CCD states that creditors have to assess the consumer's creditworthiness on the basis of sufficient information obtained from the consumer, not through information exchanges. Only where it is necessary, financial institutions have to make such assessment on the basis of a consultation of the relevant database, such circumstance occurring in those Member States whose legislation requires them to consult databases, usually a requirement that may be imposed by central banks for purposes of financial stability (see the relevant sub-heading below in this Section).

At the same time, in the following Article 9 the CCD is concerned that for competition purposes access is ensured on a non-discriminatory basis for creditors from other Member States to databases used in another Member State, if any.

Likewise, the MCD reflects the provisions of the CCD, requiring financial institutions to obtain information directly from the consumer, with the addition of relevant internal or external sources but without explicating information exchanges among lenders as the 'external source' to be used.

As for the CCD, the MCD looks at the competition side of the market and it provides for the non-discriminatory access for all creditors to the databases used in another Member States via the exchange of information among the competing creditors, specifying that such databases comprise databases operated by private information providers as well as public registers.[21]

Importantly, both the CCD and the MCD state that such provisions are without prejudice to the application of the EU data protection law on the protection of individuals with regard to the processing of personal data and on the free movement of such data, whose provisions must be respected, particularly as far as the requirements of necessity and proportionality are concerned.

Thus, against such policy and legal context the exchange of consumers' financial information and the use of centralised databases are regarded by the financial industry not only as an assessment of consumers' creditworthiness for risk management, but also as a tool to identify the over-indebtedness of individuals.

If on the one hand this industry point of view may support an argument for the exchange of information for the benefit of consumers, on the other hand it remains open to debate whether the design of databases is proportionate to the policy goals to be achieved, and whether the level of aggregation or detail of information exceeds the purpose for its sharing. Whilst the first issue raises debates over duties and social responsibilities, prudential supervision, and the institutions which should be entrusted to exercise such a public function and therefore it exceeds the

---

[21] See Articles 18, 20 and 21 of the MCD.

scope of this work,[22] in contrast the type and the level of aggregation of information, and the role of information providers bear elements relevant to competition law and policy, and they will be addressed later. From the point of view of competition and the creation of a level playing field in the EU market, all what the law says is that, if and to the extent that an information exchange takes place in a given Member State, this should occur on a non-discriminatory basis for those based in another Member State.

2.4   Securitisation

It is beyond the scope of this work to enter into discussions on the many complexities of the financial system.[23] For the purpose of information pooling and sharing, however, it is worth a mention the securitisation on lenders' portfolios of consumer loans, including mortgages.

In its simplest form, securitisation is a financial operation used by a financial institution on the receiving end of credit repayments from customers who have taken out financing. It bundles its loans repackaging the monthly loan payments into securities rated by rating agencies, and it backs them using the underlying loans as collaterals. It then transfers or sells such securities on to investors in order to receive funding which can be used to issue more loans.

This mechanism of 'securitisation' has allowed the development of new business models in the market of loans for consumers. For example, it may be used also by financial firms that are not banks, which may finance their operations not with the deposits of customers but by borrowing the money in the market which, in turn, will be used to fund loans and which they will repay back as they securitise the loans selling them on to investors.

According to financial theory, investors in asset backed securities need information on the quality of the underlying assets. Without such information, investors would not risk investing or they would require a risk premium which would signify higher refinancing costs for lenders, ultimately being passed on consumers with higher borrowing costs. Therefore, financial institution involved in the process of securitisation avail themselves of the services of credit rating agencies such as Standard and Poor's, Moody's and Fitch (only to mention the three big rating agencies that dominate the market and take the titles in the media) which grade or score the repackaged loans on the credit risk associated with those securities. In such rating of securities for the calculation of the risk of default, the agencies need to rely on data on the underlying loans from the information providers organising the exchange of information among the competing lenders. However, they do not

---

[22] Ferretti (2010), pp. 1–27.

[23] For a detailed account of the securitisation of consumer loans see, for example, Engel and McCoy (2011).

have access to the data and they need to rely on the credit score assigned by the same information providers.[24] Thus, the whole process mostly relies on a double scoring or rating from different intermediaries.

So, in a way, information exchanges and data pooling become a tool at the service of financial markets for financial operations that have repercussions on the real economy through the availability of more credit. At the same time, they may be used to feed financial products or operations that have the effect of transferring credit risks to investors, releasing lenders from concerns over defaults, and ultimately resulting in more reckless credit for consumers as well as dangers for the health and stability of the financial system. Securitisation was pointed as the biggest factor contributing to the subprime lending boom and bust which generated what is known as 'the great financial crisis' that erupted in 2008.[25]

2.5 Scoring

Credit scoring is a related, yet distinct, use of personal financial information that avails itself of ad hoc technologies which add additional features and integrate credit data with other data sources. Scoring models are mathematical algorithms or statistical programmes that determine the probable repayments of debts by consumers, assigning a score to an individual based on the information processed from a number of data sources and categorising credit applicants according to risk classes. They involve data mining techniques which include statistics, artificial intelligence, machine learning, and other fields aiming at getting knowledge from large databases.[26]

The use of scoring systems derives from so-called 'decision theory', a mathematical discipline that models people's decision-making in many areas of social activities. It is concerned with the study of how to make ideal or optimal decisions ('how people should make decisions'): in so doing, it assumes an ideal decision-maker who is fully rational, informed and able to compute with perfect accuracy. Thus, the practical application of this area of studies is concerned with the development of systematic and comprehensive tools, methodologies and software to help people to make better decisions (known as 'decision-support systems').

Behavioural decision theory has been subject to several criticisms for its numerous fallacies, particularly for introducing new biases, or for making assumptions that lack universal acceptance or that may work on large numbers but not for individual cases.[27]

---

[24] European Commission (2009); Keys et al. (2008); Engel and McCoy (2011).

[25] Ibid.

[26] See, for example, Bigus (1996); Desai et al. (1997), pp. 323–346; Handzic et al. (2003), pp. 97–109; Jensen (1992), pp. 15–26; Yobas and Crook (2000), pp. 111–125.

[27] For all see, for example, Poulton (1994).

In the end, scoring is essentially a classification and profiling technique, a way of recognising different groups in a population according to certain features expressed by a combination of personal financial and other non-personal data, which differentiates consumers on grounds of parameters and classifications set a priori from statistics for a predictive purpose.

When used to assess consumers, it is principally a way of recognising different groups in a population according to certain features, expressed by a combination of personal information and other non-personal data, and differentiating them on grounds of parameters and classifications set a priori from statistics for a predictive purpose. It is an analysis of customer behaviour having the objective to classify them in two or more groups based on a predictive outcome associated with each customer. The probability of given events, such as for example a default in the repayment of a loan, is assumed to depend on a number of characteristics of the individuals[28] The factors relevant for such a classification purpose are usually determined through an analysis of consumers' past payment history together with other descriptive information provided in the credit application form and other data from a number of different sources.

In short, the goal of credit scoring systems in the lending process is that of predicting the creditworthiness of consumers and the profitability of lenders over each one of them. It is now used for all consumer credit operations, in issuing credit cards and managing accounts, as well as in mortgage origination and securitisation operations of consumer loans. Although credit scoring was originally employed to seek to minimise the percentage of consumers who default, lenders are now using them to identify the customers who are most profitable and to maximise profits through risk based pricing according to their profile so obtained, blurring this all with direct marketing activities.[29]

2.6 Stability of the Financial System and Prudential Supervision

Information exchanges among competing lenders may be justified and used for the supervision of the financial system as a whole.

Financial prudential supervision encompasses a number of complex issues and elements that are beyond the scope of this work. Nonetheless, among the tools to achieve it, there is the need for the authorities in charge of this public function to have adequate and timely information about the behaviour, leverage, and condition of banks vis-à-vis the whole system. Among the many types of information needed by the authorities—such as asset quality, capital adequacy, liquidity, internal systems of control and security, income and dividends, foreign operations, and so

---

[28] Fractal Analytics (2003).

[29] Thomas (2000), pp. 149–172.

on—it is included the regular reporting on past due loans and non-performing loans. This not only allows supervisors to be in control and have the information on the condition and performance of the supervisees to intervene in time in case of problems, but it also constitutes an instrument to promote transparency to favour greater reliance on market discipline. Banks benefit from supervision in that they are provided with the instruments to control the quality of their loans in their daily operations. To favour this, centralised databases managed by public authorities provide banks and supervisors with aggregate information about the level of indebtedness of borrowers vis-à-vis the whole system.[30]

This mechanism relies on information exchanges among competing financial institutions where the public authority acts as the third-party pooling, aggregating, and elaborating the information exchanged, as well as the organisation setting the rules of the information exchanges.

The exchange of private financial information in this context may become clearer below in the discussion of the information providers and their role which, in turn, will later result helpful for matters of competition law and policy.

2.7 Information Providers and Policy Objectives in the EU

Credit bureaus are third-party public or private entities that provide shared negative and/or positive information to lenders in an organised form and manage centralised databases. They now exist in all EU Member States with the exception of Luxembourg, but their legal form or institutional structure varies depending on different policy or other objectives, and the function that they perform in the economy and society. Databases are organised and the types of information are provided depending on the pursuit of defined policy objectives or other private interests that they are meant to address. As noted earlier, examples of policy objectives are the stability of the financial system or the fight against over-indebtedness of consumers. Private interests, by contrast, encompass risk-management tools in the self-interest of the industry.

The distinction of the role of credit information providers reveals a key distinction between public and private or commercial organisations. While the former is normally a part of a national central bank or supervisory authority, and institutionally and legally designed to address the stability of the financial system and the monitoring of the indebtedness of consumer households, the latter offers to the market risk-management and market intelligence tools to enhance economic

---

[30] Jappelli and Pagano (2000, 2003), pp. 81–114; Jappelli and Pagano (2006), pp. 347–371; Ferretti (2008); Brealey et al. (2001), sp. Chap. 2; Cartwright (2004), sp. 31–34; Lastra (1996); Lastra and Shams (2001), pp. 165–188.

efficiency and the profitability of financial institutions irrespective of whether these are banks lending the money of depositors or any other entity doing business through the provision of credit in return for profit.[31]

2.7.1 Private or Commercial Information Providers

Private or commercial information providers are also known as Credit Reference Agencies or Credit Bureaus depending on the jurisdiction of reference. Nevertheless, the terms 'Agency' (when reference is made to Credit Reference Agencies) or 'Bureau' (when the locution Credit Bureau is used) are misleading historical ones that have attained the force of custom. In fact, despite they may suggest a publicly supervised information system, these organisations are fully-fledged privately owned companies working for profit that are no more controlled, monitored, or influenced by State-controlled organisations or other public bodies than any other privately owned organisation or business. Nor are they accountable to public bodies, central banks, or other financial service regulators, as the case may be.

Indeed, the main feature of private information providers is that they are companies that are subject to the same rules and regulations as every business in the marketplace. Their job is to provide services to the financial services industry compiling databases that the latter can access to help them in evaluating a (potential) consumer's credit application, ultimately sharing information within the industry about consumer borrowers. They can have a broad range of client members depending on the jurisdiction, from banks to non-bank lenders. In addition to traditional financing firms that are not banks, other less obvious examples may include telecommunication companies, utility companies, mail order companies, and/or any other business advancing goods or services to consumers paying for them at a later stage. Consultation of their databases is not mandatory by law prior to the underwriting of credit and is carried out on a voluntary basis. As participation by lenders in a privately owned consumer credit information system is not compulsory, the rules relating to the functioning of the system are not imposed by law or regulation but are contracted in a typical supplier-client relationship. The negotiating power of a lender changes from country to country depending on a number of factors, including for example competition in that market and/or maturity of the system, i.e., whether the information provider is

---

[31] Jappelli and Pagano (2003), pp. 81–114, Jappelli and Pagano (2006), pp. 347–371; Ferretti (2008). The state of affairs in Europe appears to be a mixed one: while in Belgium and France only public entities operate, in Denmark, Estonia, Finland, Greece, Cyprus, Hungary, Ireland, Malta, The Netherlands, Poland, Sweden, and the UK the business of information providers has been left to free market forces. In some Member States, however, private and public Credit Registries coexist (Austria, Bulgaria, Czech Republic, Germany, Italy, Latvia, Lithuania, Portugal, Romania, Slovakia, Slovenia, and Spain).

a start-up activity with no or little client members or a well-established one with wide market participation, as well as other conceivable situations in the between.

The credit data collected and processed are supplied to the centralised database by the lenders themselves, who in this way exchange information and build the database itself. By way of contractual agreement, the information is supplied by the lenders on a reciprocal basis, i.e. the lenders are able to access the databases only if they contribute to it for the benefit of all the other contributing member lenders. The reciprocity mechanism, also known as 'reciprocity principle', is key in contractual agreements between information suppliers and financial institutions as it builds the databases and it impacts on comprehensiveness, hence on accuracy.

As it has been reported in recent years, however, a number of lenders themselves have become concerned that such arrangements on 'reciprocity' are gradually breaking down. There are doubts and different practices concerning the interpretations of what exactly would constitute the 'reciprocal supply and use of data', since personal data are now processed, communicated, and analysed with sophistication that no one imagined when data sharing schemes were first established more or less 30 years ago.[32] The technological change and growth in the number and range of techniques used today, as well as secondary uses associated with credit information, such as consumer risk scoring (which includes both behavioural and sociological customer scoring), loan or mortgage rating, risk screening, monitoring, propensity modelling, debtor tracking, and support to debt collection, were not in place when the industry first began to consider the exchange of information as an instrument built for lending purposes. All such uses make it difficult to conceive a contribution of data by lenders on a reciprocal basis every time they take advantage of the information supplied. In addition, it may be worth noting that it is not always easy to draw the line and make a distinction between the use of consumers data for actual credit risk management and their use for marketing purposes, nor is there a law or regulation specifically designed to restrict new business sectors or government agencies as potential future data users and suppliers as client members of private Credit Bureaus. All these examples, in the end, make the real application of the reciprocity principle difficult or, in cases, non-transparent. At least, they may show the conflicting interests of commercial ventures to rigidly abide by it.

In some jurisdictions where they operate, then, databases may be supplemented by non-credit data collected from other sources. Thus, financial and non-financial entities may have access to consumer information across different economic segments. In this way, accessibility to full credit and other non-credit data become capable of affecting the inclusion, exclusion, or sorting in different economic spheres of the consumers.

Private information providers also supply their clients with related additional services, in particular credit scoring services by which they rate borrowers

---

[32] Hurst (1998), sp. 28.

according to their credit history and profile derived from the processing of information from different data sources. Where a wide range of data is available, the models may be intensively and increasingly used for purposes other than the assessment of borrowers' creditworthiness, for example scoring customers to promote financial products, price loans, manage credit limits, etc.

As matter of fact, all these activities are business intelligence or marketing activities that help lenders to segment the market and the client base and price loans. As an illustration, this is also the instrument used to sort consumers in prime and sub-prime borrowers.

2.7.2 Public Information Providers

Public credit bureaus (also sometimes referred as 'public credit registries') are institutions typical of continental Europe, where they first originated and developed with the objective of providing an information system for supervisors to analyse banks portfolios and monitor the health and soundness of the overall financial system of a country, as well as the level of indebtedness of borrowers, both legal and natural persons.

The Committee of Governors of the European Central Bank defines them as information systems "designed to provide commercial banks, central banks, and other regulatory bodies with information about the indebtedness of firms and individuals vis-à-vis the whole banking system".[33]

From the definition above, it emerges that the information collected by public Credit Bureaus serves mainly two purposes: (i) to conduct the prudential supervision of banks, monitoring the health and soundness of the overall financial system of a country; and (ii) to assess and monitor the indebtedness of borrowers, both legal and natural persons.

The first purpose means that they exercise a public function by furthering the general stability of the banking and payment system. As they respond to the need for safeguarding the financial stability of the national system, this requires the monitoring of the safety and soundness of banks, which includes the monitoring of the amount of exposure of each bank towards legal persons and individuals who, consequently, undergo checks over their levels of indebtedness.

This function is referred as 'prudential supervision' to emphasise the 'prudence' needed to manage banks, because—in very simple terms - banks collect and hold peoples' savings and deposits, they are a vital source of credit for businesses, and they manage the payments system.

Only banks participate in the system and are subject to the underlying rules, unlike private registries that are conceived as open systems with the incentive of bringing an increasing number of subscribers and information into play.

---

[33] Jappelli and Pagano (2003), pp. 81–114.

Also in this case there is a two-way flow of customers' credit information between lenders and the centralised database. The first flow is from the participating institutions to the public bureau. The latter, in turn, consolidates the data on the loans granted to the same borrower by each bank in order to obtain the total indebtedness, thus reporting the aggregate indebtedness. This means that unlike private information providers, public credit bureaus have universal coverage of all loans above a threshold amount determined by law or regulation and the information consists of credit data disseminated in a consolidated form. Lenders have access to the total loan exposure of each borrower, there is no detail on individual loans, and no merger with other personal data or data mining occurs. Public providers operate under strict confidentiality for participating banks and the data provided by banks are disseminated in aggregate form. No secondary uses, data mining, or data manipulation are attached to the system.[34]

Another key difference is that financial institutions that are under the supervision of a country's central bank or supervisory authority are required to report certain credit data on a regular basis by law or other regulation. As participation in the system is compulsory, its rules are imposed by law or regulation and not under contract. This compulsory nature also means that public bureaus have complete coverage of the financial institutions of a country, and no bank lenders are left out as may happen when parties are free to negotiate whether to take part in a system or not, or which system to be part of if more than one exists.[35]

Equally, public authorities have a legal basis for demanding that reporting lenders remedy possible inaccuracies or make available missing data. Failure to comply can result in sanctions that may be imposed by law, such as penalty fees followed by supervisory actions.[36]

Such mandatory reporting and rules of participation represent a fundamental difference between public and private information providers and they have a decisive impact on the legal framework of the relevant information systems.

The above differences between private/commercial and public Credit Bureaus have induced some to argue that rather than being simple substitutes, the two type of information providers seem to be complimentary parts of a country's whole credit reporting or information exchange system for the retail financial sector.[37]

It seems undisputable from all the features discussed above that private or commercial Credit Bureaus on the one side, and public Credit Bureaus on the other side cannot be reciprocally substitutes to the extent that the latter exercise functions in the public interest that the former are not entitled and do not perform. Public providers, however, can substitute for private/commercial ventures to the extent that the lenders' debt provisioning remains tightly controlled and the amount of overdue or defaulted debt is controlled. When a borrower that deals

---

[34] Jappelli and Pagano (2003), pp. 81–114; Ferretti (2008).

[35] Ibid.

[36] Miller (2003b), pp. 25–79.

[37] Ibid. See also Jentzsch (2005).

with a bank is already indebted, the public bureau sends to the concerned lender the borrower's aggregate position vis-à-vis the entire banking system.

On the contrary, whether private or commercial information providers can legitimately be considered complimentary to the public ones is doubtful and open to debate. This question raises difficult questions and complex legal issues such as, for example, the relevance, adequacy, and compliance of the existing legal framework with the arrangements and mechanisms in place or the design of the databases to address the functions that they aim to perform.

2.7.3 The Fragmented Picture Across the EU

The result is a fragmented and significantly diverse picture across the EU.

Tables 2.1, 2.2 and 2.3 summarise at a glance such a fragmentation described earlier. They show profound differences in the legal form and structure in the various Member States, the different roles of credit bureaus, and the various types of data exchanged.

Certainly, the traditional absence of European market integration in consumer finance, coupled with differences in cultures, traditions, organisation, institutions, and laws have contributed markedly to the uneven development and multi-layered segmentation of consumer information exchange systems within the EU.

But the above is corroborated by different legal forms, functions, and role of credit bureaus in the various Member States, as well as the different type or nature of information that are exchanged, which vary considerably from jurisdiction to jurisdiction in the EU.

Indeed, another important feature that may be observed from such a fragmented picture concerns the differences in the type of information collected from Member State to Member State.

The majority of credit bureaus, either public or private, collect and disseminate both positive and negative information; by contrast, a fewer, but still significant, number of them limit the collection and dissemination to only the negative information.[38]

---

[38] Negative information usually refers to data about defaults on payments, delays, delinquencies, bankruptcies etc. That is, information with a negative connotation on the payment history and the financial behaviour of the consumer. Positive information, by contrast, refers to data with a positive connotation, such as data about the financial standing, payments and other details which do not indicate a default or a late payment. Attempts have also been made to classify information which refers to data on accounts which demonstrate some signs of problems but have not yet proceeded to the state of being negative, i.e. accounts which are in acceptable time arrears with no warning to the customer being yet issued by the lender. Usually, these categorisations vary from Member State to Member State.

Table 2.1 Legal form and structure of credit bureaus in the Member States of the EU

Country	Public credit register	No. of private credit bureaus			Ownership structure		
		For profit	Not for profit	Not ownership by credits	≤50 % ownership by creditors	>50 % ownership by creditors	Other
Austria	Yes		1				1
Belgium	Yes						
Bulgaria	Yes	1		1			
Cyprus	No	1				1	
Czech Rep.	Yes	1			1		
Denmark	No	2		2			
Estonia	No	1		1			
Finland	No	1		1			
France	Yes						
Germany	Yes	1			1		
Greece	No	1			1		
Hungary	No	1			1		
Ireland	No	1			1		
Italy	Yes	2	1	1		1	1
Latvia	Yes						
Lithuania	Yes	1				1	
Luxembourg	No						
Malta	No	1				1	
Netherlands	No	1	1	1			1
Poland	No	1		–	1	–	
Portugal	Yes	2				1	
Romania	Yes	2		1	1		
Slovakia	Yes	2		1	1		
Slovenia	Yes		1				1
Spain	Yes	2		1		1	
Sweden	No	6		5	1		
United Kingdom	No	3		3			

Source European Parliament (2011), European Commission (2009)

Table 2.2   Role and structure of private/commercial and public credit bureaus

	Credit bureau	Public credit register
Ownership structure	Private/commercial entity	Central Bank or Supervisory Authority
Clients structure	Mainly creditors but sometimes also other services providers	Financial institutions authorised to grant credit
Scope	Credit assessment and monitoring	Banking supervision, building statistics, financial stability studies
		Monitoring and preventing over-indebtedness
		Credit assessment
		Fostering credit institutions prudent management
Creditors' participation	Generally voluntary	Mandatory by law
Principle of reciprocity/Non discriminatory access	Yes	Yes
Type of data stored	Full credit data (positive and negative data)	Credit data from financial institutions authorised to grant credit (including both positive and negative data in a majority of cases)
	Often also non-credit data	Data on bankruptcy of natural and legal persons
Additional services provided to creditors	Mainly:	None
	Credit scoring based on the whole CB dataset	
	Software applications	
	Portfolio management services	
	Fraud prevention systems	
	Authentication products…	
Use of thresholds	Yes, but generally low	Yes
Degree of detail of the information provided[17]	Detailed information on each individual loan. In some countries, credit information merged with other data (e.g. from public sources)	Information sometimes in a consolidated form (giving the total loan exposure of each borrower). In some PCRs, (Belgium, Italy, Portugal or Spain), the information is also given in a detailed form
Coverage	Depends on the legislation, length of service provided, financial culture, etc.	Universal coverage

Source European Commission (2009)

Table 2.3 Type of information and operations in the Member States of the EU

Country	Data structure				Threshold (€)		CBs operations			
	PCR		CB		PCR	CB	For creditors only	For creditors + other service providers	For credit assessment only	For other purposes
	Positive and negative	Negative only	Positive and negative	Negative only						
Austria	•		•		3,5000		•		•	•
Belgium	•				200					
Bulgaria	•		•				•		•	•
Cyprus			•							
Czech Rep.	•		•				•		•	
Denmark				•					•	
Estonia			•							
Finland				•			•	•	•	•
France		•			500					
Germany	•ᵃ		•		1,5 ML	100	•	•	•	•
Greece			•				•		•	
Hungary			•				•		•	
Ireland			•				•		•	
Italy	•		•	•	30,000ᵇ		•		•	
Latvia	•				150					

(continued)

Table 2.3 (continued)

Country	Data structure				Threshold (€)		CBs operations			
	PCR		CB		PCR	CB	For creditors only	For creditors + other service providers	For credit assessment only	For other purposes
	Positive and negative	Negative only	Positive and negative	Negative only						
Lithuania	•			•						
Luxembourg										
Malta				•						
Netherlands			•				•		•	
Poland			•		50	125	•		•	
Portugal	•		•				•		•	
Romania	•		•				•		•	
Slovakia	•		•				•	•	•	
Slovenia			•				•			
Spain	•		•		6,000		•	•	•	
Sweden			•				•	•	•	•
United Kingdom			•				•	•	•	•

Note[a] Does not cover consumers, [b] No threshold applies to bad debts
Source European Parliament (2011), European Commission (2009)

The type of information exchanged represents a very important feature in the design of an information exchange system, and it may as well carry with it implications for the interoperability of systems within the EU.

In turn, it will be seen later, this may have implications for competition law and policy, the protection of European consumers, and the safeguard of their fundamental rights.

2.8 Concluding Remarks

This Chapter has shown that there are a variety of purposes or rationales for exchanging consumer financial information.

Theoretical economic studies have focused on the market intelligence and competition side of information exchanges for the retail financial industry, but conclusive evidence of cause and effect between past behaviour and failure to repay debts of consumers does not exist. Moreover, the empirical evidence available or cited by the literature is scarce, it lacks transparency, and it appears thin to fully support the advanced economic theory. Nevertheless, risk assessment and decision making are important for retail finance providers but they remain own market intelligence and strategies of market players. It should be clear, however, that these are activities for the legitimate pursuit of profitability and carried out in the self-interest of the industry.

However, other reasons or justifications for exchanging consumer financial information exist beyond economic theory and the self-interest of the industry.

Indeed, consumer information may be exchanged to address defined public policy objectives. However, under these circumstances public goals inform the legal form of the information providers or the databases, as well as the regulation of the information exchange.

By contrast, where information exchanges make the commercial interest of the industry for market intelligence or, generally, profitability purposes, private or commercial credit bureaus operate in the marketplace as any other business venture.

In the EU, however, this distinction is often blurred or confused despite the net differentiation between clearly identified policy objectives on the one side, and the commercial interest of the credit industry on the other side.

Commercial credit bureaus cannot be substitutes of public bureaus for the different functions that they perform. However, to some extent public providers may substitute the commercial ones for the control of consumer debt levels, serving creditworthiness purposes. The inclusion of consumer financial data, in an appropriately regulated form, in public credit registries may be used not only to strengthen bank supervision but could also serve to improve the quality of credit analysis by financial institutions to the extent that this is necessary for the general interest of financial stability and the monitoring of the indebtedness of the individuals towards the system. On a micro-economic level, lenders would be able to detect and tightly control their credit provisioning and the amount of overdue and defaulted debt in circulation, whilst the public authority in charge would be allowed to supervise and control the level of indebtedness on a macro-economic basis.[39]

At the same time, the complementarity of the two is debatable, especially in light of the balancing of other consumer interests or rights which will be explored in the following Chapters.

The next Chapter, in particular, will look at the exchange of information from the perspective of traditional competition policy and law.

References

Admati AA, Pfleiderer PC (2000) Forcing firms to talk: financial disclosure regulation and externalities. Rev Financ Stud 13:479–519

Akelof G (1970) The market for 'lemons': quality uncertainty and the market mechanism. Q J Econ 28(3):523–547

Alary D, Gollier C (2001) Strategic default and penalties on the credit market with potential judgment errors. EUI Working Paper. European University Institute, Florence

Barron M, Staten S (2000) The value of comprehensive credit reports: lesson from the US experience. Research paper—credit research centre. Georgetown University, Washington D.C.

Barron M, Staten S (2003) The value of comprehensive credit reports: lesson from the us experience. In: Miller MJ (ed) Reporting systems and the international economy. MIT Press, Cambridge, pp 273–310

Berger AN, Udell GF (1995) Relationship lending and lines of credit in small firm finance. J Bus 68:351–381

Bertola G, Disney R, Grant C (2006a) The economics of consumer credit demand and supply. In: Bertola G, Disney R, Grant C (eds) The economics of consumer credit. The MIT Press, Cambridge, pp 1–26

Bertola G, Disney R, Grant C (2006b) The economics of consumer credit demand and supply. In: Bertola G, Disney R, Grant C (eds) The economics of consumer credit. The MIT Press, Cambridge, pp 347–371

Bigus JP (1996) Data mining with neural networks: solving business problems from application development to decision support. McGraw Hill, New York

Brealey RA, Clark A, Goodhart C, Healy J, Hoggarth G, Llewllyn DT et al (2001) Financial stability and central banks. Routledge, London

Cartwright P (2004) Banks, consumers and regulation. Hart Publishing, Oxford

Desai VS, Convay DG, Crook JN, Overstree GA (1997) Credit scoring models in the credit union improvement using neural networks and genetic algorithms. IMA J Math Appl Bus Ind 8:323–346

Diamond DW (1991) Monitoring and reputation: the choice between bank loans and directly placed debt. J Polit Econ 99(4):689–721

Engel KC, McCoy PA (2011) The subprime virus. Oxford University Press, Oxford

European Commission (2009) Report of the expert group on credit histories. Brussels

---

[39] For similar considerations about the value of public credit registries see also Majinoni et al. (2004).

European Parliament (2011) Responsible lending—barriers to competition, DG for internal policies, economic and monetary affairs, IP/A/ECON/ST/2011-05. European Parliament, Brussels

Ferretti F (2008) The law and consumer credit reporting systems in the ec. Routledge-Cavendish, London

Ferretti F (2010) A European perspective on consumer loans and the role of credit registries: the need to reconcile data protection, risk management, efficiency, over-indebtedness, and a better prudential supervision of the financial system. J Consum Policy 33(1):1–27

Fractal Analytics (2003) Comparative analysis of classification techniques. A Fractal Whitepaper

Giannetti C, Jentzsch N, Spagnolo G (2010) Information-sharing and cross-border entry in European banking. ECRI research report N. 11. Brussels

Handzic M, Tjandrawibawa F, Jeo J (2003) How neural networks can help loan officers to make better informed application decisions. Inform Sci 97–109

Hurst P (1998) Sharing performance data through credit reference agencies—levelling the playing field. Credit Manag 28

Jappelli T, Pagano M (2000)Information sharing in credit markets: the European experience. Working paper no. 35, centres for studies in economics and finance. University of Salerno, Salerno

Jappelli T, Pagano M (2002) Information sharing, lending and defaults: cross-country evidence. J Bank Finance 26(10):2017–2045

Jappelli T, Pagano M (2003) Public credit information: a European perspective. In: Miller MJ (ed) Reporting systems and the international economy. The MIT Press, Cambridge, pp 81–114

Jappelli T, Pagano M (2006) The role and effects of credit information sharing. In: Bertola G, Disney R, Grant C (eds) The economics of consumer credit. The MIT Press, Cambridge, pp 347–371

Jensen HL (1992) Using neural networks for credit scoring. Manag Finance 18(6):15–26

Jentzsch N (2005) Best world practices in credit reporting and data protection: lessons from China. Paper prepared for the international workshop on household credit. Peking University and University of Virginia

Keys BJ, Mukherjee TK, Seru A, Vig V (2008) Did securitization lead to lax screening? Evidence from subprime loans. Working paper prepared for the European Finance Association, Athens

Klein DB (1992) Promise keeping in great society: a model of credit information sharing. Econ Polit 4(2):117–136

Klein DB (1997) Promise keeping in the great society: a model of credit information sharing. In: Klein DB (ed) Reputation: studies in the voluntary elicitation of good conduct. University of Michigan Press, Ann Arbor, pp 267–288

Lastra RM (1996) Central banking and banking regulation. Financial Markets Group LSE, London

Lastra RM, Shams H (2001) Public accountability in the financial sector. In: Ferran E, Goodhart C (eds) Regulating financial services and markets in the twenty first century. Hart Publishing, Oxford, pp 165–188

Majinoni G, Miller M, Mylenko N, Powell A (2004) Improving credit information, bank regulation and supervision: on the role and design of public credit registries. World Bank Research Committee, Washington D.C

Miller MJ (2003a) Introduction. In: Miller MJ (ed) Reporting systems and the international economy. The MIT Press, Cambridge, pp 1–23

Miller MJ (2003b) Credit reporting systems around the globe: the state of the art in public credit registry and private credit reporting firms. In: Miller MJ (ed) Reporting systems and the international economy. The MIT Press, Cambridge, pp 25–79

Poulton EC (1994) Behavioural decision theory. Cambridge University Press, Cambridge

Riestra ASJ (2002) Credit bureaus in today's credit markets. ECRI research report no. 4. European Credit Research Institute, Brussels

Stiglitz JE, Weiss A (1981) Credit rationing in markets with imperfect information. Am Econ Rev 71(3):393–410

Thomas LC (2000) A survey of credit and behavioural scoring: forecasting financial risk of lending to consumers. Int J Forecast 16(2):149–172

Yobas M, Crook NJ (2000) Credit scoring using neural and evolutionary techniques. IMA Stat Financ Math Appl Bus Ind 11:111–125

Chapter 3
Information Exchanges Under EU Competition Law

The determination of the legitimacy or illegitimacy of exchanging consumer financial information under EU competition law finds its roots in a traditionally controversial and grey area of competition law enforcement. In addition, the financial services sector has been historically protected from the logics and application of competition law, which only relatively recently has featured importantly in the competition policies and law enforcement of the EU and its competent authorities.

On the basis of the traditional case-law of the judiciary and guidance offered by the European Commission, there are no general and theoretical rules to distinguish between a legitimate and an illegitimate exchange of information. By contrast, the determination between the two depends on the type of information exchanged, the level of aggregation, the frequency, purpose and accuracy, and the concentration of the underlying market. Generally, the analysis has to consider the economic context in which the participants to the exchange operate and establish whether this has the potential to limit competition. If it does, to be granted an exemption this must have a predominantly positive effect for consumers.

3.1 Background: The General Framework and Goals of Competition Law in Consumer Finance

"Competitive financial services markets that serve European consumers and businesses efficiently contribute to economic growth and, therefore, to the achievement of the Lisbon goals".[1]

---

[1] European Commission "Report on the retail banking sector inquiry" Commission Staff Working Document accompanying the Communication from the Commission—Sector Inquiry under Art 17 of Regulation 1/2003 on retail banking (Final Report) [COM(2007) 33 final] SEC(2007) 106.

© The Author(s) 2014
F. Ferretti, *EU Competition Law, the Consumer Interest and Data Protection*, SpringerBriefs in Law, DOI 10.1007/978-3-319-08906-5_3

The above statement is the opening remark of the European Commission's 'Report on the retail banking sector inquiry', where sector enquiries play a key role in the modernised approach to competition policy now taken in the EU.

That banks and other financial service providers are of special importance to the real economy and economic growth is certainly not a novelty. The health of the financial sector is central of any properly functioning market system and its financing, and financial institutions are the intermediaries that make the system work. Retail financial service providers deliver, among other things, the financing of consumers and small and medium enterprises (SMEs). Also, in a market economy, financial products or services become particularly sensitive for consumers as they may positively or negatively determine their everyday life, impacting on the quality of life of people, and ultimately that of society generally.

By contrast, for a number of reasons, for a long time the competitive element of financial markets and their subjectivity to the application of competition policy and law has not been straightforward nor noticeable. On the one side, this is because historically for what has been defined as their 'quasi-social' nature the financial services sector was a state prerogative, particularly in continental Europe, where state controls or monopolies gradually gave way to the market only with the establishment of the European Community and the goal of market integration.[2] On the other side, the financial sector has long been exempted from the application of competition policy and law for their perceived potential detrimental impact on financial stability, as well as for the complexities deriving from the nature itself of financial products and services, including the direct exposure to retail customers.[3]

In line with the growing academic literature, financial services are no longer an exception in the application and enforcement of competition law.[4] Despite the inherent imperfection of competition in financial services for the interlinked nature of the financial sector and the importance of its agents for stability and the economy, competition policy and law are now taken seriously and they are perceived by policy-makers as a support for the good functioning of financial markets and a guide for the identification of failures and dysfunctions.[5]

Habitually, under the teachings of the influential 'Chicago School', the main function of competition law is considered to be the safeguard and the promotion of the competitive process of undertakings, encouraging an optimum allocation of resources and efficient and innovative financial services, and ultimately enhancing consumer welfare.[6]

---

[2] Lista (2013).

[3] Carletti and Vives (2008, 2009).

[4] E.g. see Carletti (2009), pp. 449–482; Carletti and Vives (2008, 2009), Beck, et al. (2006), pp. 1581–1603; Beitel et al. (2004), pp. 109–140; Berger et al. (2009), pp. 99–118; Dermine (2003), pp. 31–95; Franchoo et al. (2012), pp. 345–364; Vives (1991), pp. 505–515.

[5] Almunia (2012).

[6] See e.g. Whish (2012), Monti (2007).

Yet, under EU competition law, another objective is the achievement of EU market integration, which does not necessarily coincide with efficiencies in the organisation of production and distribution.[7] This may be controversial for economists and a number of competition lawyers, but from its inception the EC Treaty has mandated interaction between competition policy objectives and other goals which can be eventually re-conducted to market integration. After all, it has not to be forgotten that the fundamental underlying purpose of the EU is the creation of a single market and the elimination of barriers to integration, including in the financial services sector. Moreover, even accepting that competition policy should aim at allocative efficiency and consumer welfare rather than forcing integration *per se*, the two goals may not necessarily be incompatible as competition plays a key role in keeping markets open.

Whatever consensus this position as to the goals to be achieved may have, an extensive body of EU competition law and cases have developed, which embrace these different objectives of competition policy.[8]

Now the Lisbon Treaty no longer includes in its Article 3 TEU competition policy as a Union goal in itself, but it nevertheless remains part of the internal market which is a central objective of the provision. Actually, Protocol 27 of the TFEU declares that the internal market includes a system in which competition is not distorted.

At the same time, Article 7 TFEU explicitly affirms that the EU must ensure consistency between its policies and activities, taking all of its objectives into account, which makes it clear that normatively other goals should be taken into account in addition to allocative efficiency.

Far from engaging into a detailed discussion, the above is to say that to the extent that the different goals of EU competition policy may be inconsistent with each other, a trade-off or balancing exercise may be needed. Social or other non-economic policies or interests may intervene, and they may not be neglected by competition enforcing authorities in considering a multitude of objectives and policies in the exercise of their powers. The debate is fervent in this area.[9]

Within this broader context and discussion, the financial services sector is no exception with the additional difficulty that the process of EU financial integration is still incomplete and far from been achieved.

As seen, a substantial part of the facilitation of the integration process is through the intertwining of the freedom of establishment of service providers, the promotion of cross-border activities, and the intensification of completion.

Competition law applies to the financial services sector in all the areas arising from Treaty rules.[10]

---

[7]   Van den Bergh and Camesasca (2006).

[8]   See, for e.g., *GlaxoSmithKline Services Unlimited v Commission* (Joined cases C-501/06 P, C-513/06 P, C-515/06 P, and C-519/06 P) [2009] ECR I-9291; *T-Mobile Netherlands and others* (Case C-8/08) ECR I-4529, [2009] 5 CMLR1701.

[9]   See further, Chap. 5.

[10]   Commission Report on Competition Policy Vol. 2, 1972, 51–57. *Zuchner v Bayerisce Vereinsbamk AG* (Case C-172/80) [1981] ECR-2021.

Broadly, it aims to control the following:

• Cartels, collusions, or any other anti-competitive practices having a distortive
  effect on the EU market (Article 101 TFEU);
• Market power, by means of abuses of a dominant position or via proposed
  mergers or acquisitions having an effect on the EU market (Article 102 TFEU
  and Regulation 139/2004 EC);
• Direct or indirect aid given by the Member States to undertakings (Article 107
  TFEU).

These areas are now usual battlegrounds in the financial services sector and cases
may cover a great number of practices or behaviours that are beyond the scope of
this work.[11]

As far as it concerns information exchange agreements or practices covered in
Chap. 2, they may be of particular interest for competition law for the potential
benefits but also the risks relating to market transparency, as well as the capability
of these agreements or practices to facilitate collusive conduct among competitors.

3.2 The Traditional Approach of EU Competition Law Under Article 101 TFEU

Debates over the legitimacy of information exchanges among competitors vis-à-
vis competition law in the EU are not new. Nonetheless, this traditionally remains
one of the most sensitive and critical area of competition law enforcement.

As a general rule, businesses must operate on the market independently of their
competitors and they should not conform, adjust or coordinate their behaviour with
that of competitors, including exchanging commercially sensitive information.[12]
Yet, questions as to what extent such exchanges should be permitted, and where to
draw a line between anti-competitive behaviour and genuine business, remain grey
and controversial areas which pose problems of legal certainty.[13]

---

[11] There are a variety of situations concerning competition issues. They can range from State Aid
in bail-out situations after the big crisis starting in 2008–2009 as well as restructuring of financial
institutions. Also, they include situations of abuses of dominant position in capital markets in
relation to access to financial data (e.g. see Commission proceedings against Thomson Reuters
Commission Decision 20 December 2012 in case COMP/654 and Standard & Poor's *Commission
Decision of 15 November 2011 in case COMP/39.592*). Another common area of investigation is
the one regarding payment systems, customer switching or interchange and interbank fees. For a
broader view of the application of competition law in the financial services sector see, Franchoo
et al. (2012), pp. 345–364; Lista (2013).

[12] See, for example, Carle and Johnsson (1998), pp. 74–84; Capobianco (2004), pp. 1247–1276;
Seitz (2011), pp. 452–462; Whish (2006), pp. 19–42. See also *DSM NW v Commission* (Case T 8/
89) [1991] ECR II-1833, para 209.

[13] See, for example, Scherer and Ross (1990), Clarke (1983), 383–394.

According to economic theory, information exchanges are not necessarily anti-competitive. On the contrary, in order to make sound decisions and planning, companies need market intelligence and information pertaining to, and shared with, competitors. Appropriate information allows them to engage in bench-marking, have efficiency gains, plan production and investments, improve their marketing, and price products competitively.[14]

On the other hand, information exchanges can be anti-competitive to the extent that they may favour concerted practices in a particular sector, or they may serve for the establishment or stabilisation of cartels. When detailed information is exchanged within an industry, it may become easier for participating undertakings to act in concert, which is contrary to the fundamental nature of competition which requires that competitors act independently and not coordinate their behaviour in the market. In this perspective, market intelligence is a competitive strength or weakness of competing firms, where those who are better have gains, at the same time forcing the others to improve if they are to remain competitive on the market.[15]

Traditionally, all the case-law on the competitive or anti-competitive nature of the exchange of information, as well as the European Commission's interpretation and enforcement, have centred on the application of Article 101 TFEU (formerly Article 81 TEC).

Articles 101(1) and (2) TFEU prohibit and void all agreements between undertakings, decisions by associations of undertakings and concerted practices which may affect, actually or potentially, trade between Member States and which have as their object or effect the prevention, restriction or distortion of competition within the internal market. Article 101(3) TFEU, in turn, exempts anti-competitive agreements, decisions or concerted practices which contribute to improving the production or distribution of goods/services, at the same time allowing consumers a fair share of such benefit—the so-called 'consumer interest'.

Prima facie, thus, any communication of information among competitors may be potentially dangerous from a competition law perspective. This is because the scope of Article 101 TFEU is broad and not only obvious anti-competitive agreements are caught by the prohibition, such as those on prices, production or

---

[14] Henry (1994), pp. 483–512; Boutler (1999), pp. 434–441; Posner (1979), pp. 1187–1203; Bennett and Collins (2010), pp. 311–337; Whish (2006), pp. 19–42; OECD (2010).

[15] This has been a long set position of the EU Commission which has viewed the exchange of information between competitors as a practice falling within the scope of Article 101 TFEU (ex 81 TEC). See, for example, the landmark Commission Decision *UK Agricultural Tractor Exchange* OJ 1992 L 68/19. It is also a well-established principle under EU competition law in the seminal cases *Thyssen Stahl AG v Commission* (Case C 194/99) [2003] ECR I-10821and *John Deere v Commission* (Case C 7/95) [1998] ECR I-3111, which affirmed that traders must determine independently their policies on the common market and their conditions to customers, strictly precluding any direct or indirect contact whose object or effect is to create abnormal conditions of competition. In so doing, the CJEU has clarified that regard has to be taken as to the nature of the products or services, the size and number of the undertakings, and the volume of the market. See also Vives (2006), pp. 83–100.

marketing limits, and market allocation. Even in the absence of any such explicit or implicit agreements, Article 101 TFEU proscribes concerted practices having as their object or effect the prevention, restriction, or distortion of competition in the internal market which is a complex determination depending largely on the facts. Where it is clear that an agreement has as its object the restriction of competition, there is no need to demonstrate the anti-competitive effects.[16]

In its most recent judgement *T-Mobile Netherlands and others*, the CJEU has taken a strict view regarding the anti-competitive object of an exchange of information, confirming that even a limited exchange between competitors concerning matters other than prices to customers and in the context of a single occasion can infringe EU competition rules.[17] By contrast, whenever the object of the agreement is not so clear an effect analysis has to be conducted to determine whether this is or should be caught by Article 101 TFEU vis-à-vis neutral or pro-competitive exchanges.

Under Article 101 TFEU, whilst the locutions 'agreement' and 'decision' pose little interpretative challenges, the meaning of what constitutes a 'concerted practice' may be more problematic.

The CJEU has held that a concerted practice is

> a form of coordination between undertakings which, without having reached the stage where an agreement properly so-called has been concluded, *knowingly substitutes practical cooperation* between them for the risks of competition.
> By its very nature, then, a concerted practice does not have all the elements of a contract but may inter alia arise out of *coordination which becomes apparent from the behaviour of the participants*.
> Conduct is such as to enable those concerned to attempt (...) to consolidate established positions to the detriment of effective freedom of movement of the products in the common market and of the freedom of consumers to choose their suppliers.[18]

Established case law specifies that for an Article 101 TFEU infringement to occur it is sufficient the existence of the wilful element (the "knowingly" above) even in the absence of actual anticompetitive effects on the market, so that it is not necessary that the conduct in fact produces the specific effect of restricting, preventing or distorting competition.[19]

As said, however, not all communications are prohibited but only the exchange of information which may have an effect on competition is incompatible with

---

[16] For all, see Capobianco (2004), pp. 124–1276. On an object analysis in information exchanges among competitors see Ortega Gonzalez (2012), pp. 1–57.

[17] In its most recent judgment in this area *T-Mobile Netherlands and others* (Case C-8/08) [2009] ECR I-4529 the CJUE took a strict view on information exchanges affirming that "an exchange of information which is capable of removing uncertainties between participants as regards the timing, extent and details of modifications to be adopted by the undertaking concerned must be regarded as pursuing an anti-competitive object".

[18] *Imperial Chemical Industries Ltd v. Commission of the European Communities* (Cases 48-69/72) [1972] ECR 619.

[19] *Hüls AG v Commission of the European Communities* (Case C–199/92 P) [1999] ECR I–4287.

Article 101(1) TFEU. As made clear in *UK Agricultural Tractor Registration Exchange*,[20] what indeed matters from an antitrust point of view is the actual exchange of confidential information, its level of aggregation, its frequency and accuracy, and the concentration of the reference market.

In fact, to be pertinent, information needs to have sensitive market value for the undertaking possessing it, as information of non-confidential nature is not an issue by definition.[21] Also, the more information is aggregated, i.e. the less detailed it is, the less hazardous it is for competition: transactions that reveal specific content are likely to be identifying, allowing the recognition of strategies of competitors or disclosing which data set belong to a specific competitor.[22]

To be compatible with competition law, information needs to be up-to-date and accurate too, as inaccurate communications may easily distort market behaviour and fairness in competition.[23] Besides, in concentrated markets, the exchange of information is more likely to lead to collusive behaviour between market players, as it is easier to identify competitors' behaviour and strategies. Secrecy and uncertainty of the behaviour or intelligence of the few players of a market may constitute the key factor left for residual competition and avoid tacit agreements or concerted practices. In addition, in a concentrated market the lack of participation in the exchange system prevents entry to new players as non-members would be penalised regardless of whether they join the system or not.[24] If they do not, in fact, they would be penalised for not having access to such information. At the same time, if they decide and they are allowed to join, they would be obliged to disclose and share with existing undertakings (i.e. their new competitors) sensitive or confidential information which, in turn, may allow the latter to avert new or aggressive market strategies by the new entrant. In case they do not have information to share, as new market entrants with no portfolio of information of the

---

[20] Cit. *supra* at note n. 15.

[21] See Commission Decision 2003/570/EC of 30 April 2003 relating to a proceeding under Article 81 of the EC Treaty and Article 53 of the EEA Agreement—Case COMP/ 38.370—*O2 UK Limited/T-Mobile UK Limited* ("UK Network Sharing Agreement") (notified under document number C(2003) 1384).

[22] For a detailed analysis of the identifying nature of information and the relevance of aggregation see von Papp (2007), pp. 264–270. According to the author, the exchange of identifying information not only stabilises collusion, but it does not have pro-competitive effects and should be considered per se prohibited.

[23] See, for example, CFI case *Wirtschaftsvereinigung Stahl* (Case T-16/98) [2001] ECR II-01217.

[24] *UK Agricultural Tractor Registration Exchange*, cit. at 15. See also European Commission's Notice concerning agreements, decisions and concerted practices in the field of co-operation between enterprises, OJ 1968, C 75/3, replaced by the Commission's Guidelines on the applicability of Article 81 to horizontal co-operation agreements, OJ 2001, C 3/2, in turn replaced by the Commission's Guidelines on the applicability of Article 101 of the Treaty on the Functioning of the European Union to horizontal co-operation agreements, OJ 2011, C 1/25; Capobianco (2004), pp. 1247–1276.

relevant market, they may well be prevented to join the system for lack of reciprocity.[25]

In its latest case *T-Mobile Netherlands and others*, the CJEU stressed particularly the significance of independent economic operators and the prominence of market concentration for the assessment of restraints on competition.[26]

From the European case-law and Commission's practice, the literature observes how on the one side the exchange of core competitive information has been treated as either enhancing or facilitating actual or potential collusive market behaviour or as an artificial enhancement of market transparency eliminating that uncertainty that is so important for competitive markets and market rivalry.[27] From another angle, on the other side, economic theory continues to stress that market transparency may be positive for the ideal model of perfect competition premised on the elimination of information asymmetry about the market itself and the benefit that this offers to new market entrants vis-à-vis existing market players. At the same time, however, there is the recognition that increased market transparency can make the market more collusive, fixing prices and/or segmenting customers (welfare reducing) rather than providing more choice or broadening market access for customers (welfare improving). The key concern with transparency is that it allows for better monitoring and more effective punishment of deviating members or non-members.[28]

In conclusion, all discussions confirm the difficulty of elaborating general and theoretical rules to distinguish between a legitimate and an illegitimate exchange of information, pointing to the need of taking an approach on a case-by-case basis encompassing the economic context in which the participants to the information exchange operate and establishing whether or not information sharing has the potential to limit competition and, in case, whether this should be exempted for its predominantly positive effects for consumers.

3.3 The Retail Financial Sector: *Asnef Equifax* v. *Ausbanc*

Against the illustrated case-by-case scenario, the position over the competitive or anti-competitive nature of information sharing holds also for the retail financial sector. A depicted pro-competitive effect of sharing knowledge over customers

---

[25] See, for example, CFI *Cement* (joined cases T-25, 26, 30, 32, 34–39, 42–46, 48, 50–65, 68–71, 87, 88, 103–104/95), [2000] ECR II-491.

[26] *T-Mobile Netherlands and others* (Case C-8/08) [2009] ECR I-4529 has been criticised for leading to further confusion in the competition law analysis of information exchanges. Commentators claim that it should not be misinterpreted as advocating a simplistic approach but, instead, it makes clear that an information exchange that is ancillary to a cartel must be treated together with the cartel, and thus as a *per se* violation. See Meyring (2009), pp. 30–32.

[27] von Papp (forthcoming); Capobianco (2004), pp. 1247–1276; Whish (2006), pp. 19–42.

[28] Ibid. In particular, see also Giannetti et al. (2010).

financial transactions is the reduction of information monopolies of large lenders, such as big mainstream banks, which not only put on the same competitive footing existing smaller competitors, but also new entrants in the market which would not enter the market or be at disadvantage pooling credit applicants previously rejected by incumbents.[29]

At EU level, this may be problematic to the extent that freedom of establishment and freedom to provide and receive services are cornerstones of the internal market. At the same time, one of the peculiarities is that this is a risk-averse industry. As seen, even though information sharing can serve strategic and competitive purposes, it is mainly used for credit risk diminution and the reduction of market uncertainty, where the main concern is to screen out or price higher risks more.

Looking at EU competition law, also in the financial services sector any assessment of the legitimacy of the exchange of consumer financial information should investigate the characteristics of the European consumer credit market against the concept of concerted practices and actual or potential anti-competitive effects, in particular against the concentration of the reference market, the regularity of the exchanges, the confidential nature and the level of aggregation of the information, as well as its accuracy.[30]

The CJEU had the opportunity to shed light on the fine line between anti-competitive behaviour and genuine business in the exchange of consumer financial information in the case *Asnef Equifax v. Ausbanc* (hereinafter *Asnef*).[31]

It concerned the circumstances in which banks could exchange information about the solvency and creditworthiness of their consumer customers. It involved a Spanish private credit bureau—i.e. not a public institution which, as seen in the previous Chapter, performs distinct and unique roles in the economy that cannot be confused with that of private or commercial information providers.

The Spanish High Court referred to the CJEU for a ruling whether such information exchange was in breach of then Article 81 TEC [now Article 101 TFEU] and, in case, whether such an agreement could be authorised by a national competition authority under then Article 81(3) TEC [now Article 101(3) TFEU] if the implementation of the agreement could benefit consumers.

The opinion of the Advocate General ('A-G') anticipated the judgement confirming that the case-law on information exchanges "does not prohibit all elimination of uncertainty generally, but only certain types of uncertainty, in particular uncertainty about the conduct of competitors on the market".[32] The A-G was of

---

[29] Van Tassel and Vishwasrao (2007), pp. 3742–3760; Giannetti et al. (2010), Carletti and Vives (2008, 2009).

[30] Commission Decision *UK Agricultural Tractor*, cit. *supra* at note n. 15.

[31] *Asnef-Equifax, Servicios de Información sobre Solvencia y Crédito, SL v Asociación de Usuarios de Servicios Bancarios (Ausbanc)* (Case C-238/05), [2006] ECR I-11125.

[32] Opinion of the Advocate General Geelhoed delivered on 29 June 2006, I 11131–11144, para 53.

the opinion that credit bureaus remove uncertainty of the solvency of customers, not of the behaviour of competitors, to favour competition.[33]

Reaffirming the principles of precedent case-law, the CJEU followed the opinion of the A-G clarifying that compatibility with EU competition law cannot be assessed in the abstract but it depends on the economic conditions on the relevant markets and on specific characteristics of the system concerned. In particular, relevance should be given to its purpose, the conditions of access and participation, the type of information exchanged, its periodicity, its importance for the fixing of prices, volumes or conditions of service, and its accuracy.[34]

In conclusion, in the first part of the judgement, the CJEU ruled that an information exchange of credit bureaus is in principle permissible if:

- Relevant markets are not highly concentrated;
- The system does not allow lenders to be identified;
- The conditions of access to the system are not discriminatory, in law or in fact.[35]

However, the Court acknowledged that, even if the object of the information exchange was not to restrict competition, it could have had the effect of doing so.[36]

In the second part of the ruling, therefore, the CJEU looked at the consumer fair share, or consumer interest, under then Article 81(3) TEC [now Article 101(3) TFEU] if the referring court finds that there is a reduction in competition. The CJEU held that the national court should focus on the consumer fair share of the profit resulting from the information exchange, which in the case at hand is that credit bureaus are capable of helping to prevent consumer over-indebtedness and overall offering a greater availability of credit, as well as of favouring the mobility of consumers.[37] All in all, in the view of the CJEU such economic advantages might be such as to offset the disadvantages of a possible restriction on competition, which is a circumstance for national courts to verify.[38]

The key determination of the 'consumer interest' was that, if some consumers pay more or they are refused credit as a result of information sharing, this cannot prevent the condition that consumers are allowed fair share of the benefit.[39] In the reasoning of the CJEU, "under Article 81(3) EC [now Article 101(3) TFEU] it is the beneficial nature of the effect on *all consumers in the relevant markets* that must be taken into consideration, not the effect on each member of that category of consumers" [emphasis added].[40] Moreover, according to the learned judges, since credit bureaus are capable of leading to a greater availability of credit, it is

---

[33] Ibid., para 52 *et seq.*

[34] *Asnef,* first part of the judgement.

[35] Ibid.

[36] Ibid. para 48, which specifies that it is for national courts to determine it.

[37] Ibid., para 67–71.

[38] Ibid., second part of the judgement.

[39] Ibid., para 69–71.

[40] Ibid., para 70.

beneficial for applicants for whom interest rates might be higher if lenders didn't know of their personal situation.[41]

The requisite of 'indispensability' of the final part of Article 101(3) was not investigated by the CJEU but it is nevertheless explicit in the provision itself and cannot be overlooked. Any restriction which satisfies the efficiency gains and the fair-share of consumers should be strictly necessary to the attainment of these objectives, and the parties will need to prove that the content, aggregation, age, confidentiality, frequency, and coverage of the exchanged data carry the lowest risk indispensable for creating the claimed gains.

Moreover, the gains attained by indispensable restrictions must be passed to consumers. According to the European Commission, the lower is the market power of the parties involved in the information exchange, the more likely it is that said gains would be passed on to consumers.[42]

Whether as a result of information sharing national credit market participants have lower market power remains debatable and it lacks demonstration. This assessment should have been subjected to an analysis that the judiciary did not address.

All the same, in the end, for the exchange of information in the financial services sector *Asnef* provides financial institutions with a precedent giving a degree of certainty over the practice of sharing consumer information in the EU, albeit negative information only. For instance, following the CJEU decision Spain approved a block exemption regulation for the exchange of information of consumer defaults.[43]

However, certainty is not synonymous with justice or righteousness. At a closer scrutiny of issues affecting personal information of individuals, the case may be criticised on a number of grounds, mostly on doubts over uncharted assumptions of the sharing of private financial information of consumers by private dominant companies, as well as misconceptions over the role of such providers in the economy. Similarly, concerns may arise over the reading of what accounts as the 'consumer interest'. These are issues that will be covered next and in the following Chapters.

3.4 Information Exchanges in the Policy and Guidelines of the European Commission

The European Commission's attention to the exchange of information among competitors has a long history dating back to the late nineteen sixties.

From the start, it was documented that it falls under the sphere of application of Article 101 TFEU (at the time the equivalent provision was Article 85 TEC). There was already the recognition that the assessment of such agreements or practices on

---

[41] Ibid. para 71.

[42] European Commission in OECD (2010), sp. 308–321.

[43] Royal Decree 602/2006 of 19 May 2006, Official State Gazette no. 129 of 31 May 2006.

the restraint of competition could vary depending on the features of a given sector and the specific facts of the case, but that a critical element for such an assessment is the existence of an oligopolistic market for homogeneous products.[44] This policy was detailed only in the aftermath of the *Sugar* case[45] making it explicit that these circumstances require a case-by-case approach. The criteria that were indicated for the assessment referred to the structure of the market facilitating the coordination of the commercial behaviour of competitors, the nature and scope of the exchange having an impact on the likelihood of coordination of market strategies rather than competition, and the private or public nature of the exchange where only the latter improve competition allowing customers to compare market offers.

As seen in the above Section, the European Commission's position was first put in practice in the assessment of the case *UK Agricultural Tractor Exchange*,[46] later confirmed by the Court of First Instance and the European Court of Justice (respectively, the General Court and the CJEU in the nomenclature post-Lisbon Treaty), and followed by other cases first above analysed in this Chapter.

In order to provide guidance on the applicability of competition law to horizontal cooperation agreements, in the belief that guidelines may promote an optimal and manageable self-assessment framework for the use of firms, in 2001 the Commission issued 'Guidelines on the applicability of Article 81 *(now Article 101 TFEU)* to horizontal co-operation agreements'.

It is significant that the exchange of information was explicitly excluded from such guiding principles, probably signifying the delicate and complex nature of such agreements or practices.

The 2001 Guidelines expressly stated that:

> The present guidelines do not, however, address all possible horizontal agreements. They are only concerned with those types of cooperation which potentially generate efficiency gains, namely agreements on R&D, production, purchasing, commercialisation, standardisation, and environmental agreements. Other types of horizontal agreements between competitors, for example on the exchange of information or on minority shareholdings, are to be addressed separately (para 10).

It is only with the adoption in 2011 of the European Commission's 'Guidelines on the applicability of Article 101 TFEU to horizontal co-operation agreements' (hereinafter '2011 Guidelines')[47] that for the first time it is included a section on the general principles on the competitive assessment of information exchanges.

---

[44] European Commission, Notice concerning Agreements, Decisions and Concerted Practices in the field of Co-operation between Enterprises, [1968] OJ C075.

[45] Commission in Decision 97/624/EC, *Irish Sugar plc*, O.J. 1997, L 258/1.

[46] Cit. *supra* at note n. 15.

[47] OJ 2011, C 1/25. In addition to the goal of increasing legal certainty, the *2011 Guidelines* purport to strengthen innovation and competitiveness as well as to minimise agreements which are anticompetitive and harmful to the industry and consumers alike. See Press Release of the European Commission, "Commission adopts revised competition rules on horizontal cooperation agreements", (14 December 2010), IP/10/1702, available at http://europa.eu/rapid/pressReleasesAction. do?reference=IP/10/1702.

By replacing the 2001 Guidelines,[48] the novelty of adding a chapter on information exchanges has been welcome by some for having been overdue and finally providing some clarity, especially by bringing together the jurisprudence first analysed in this paper.[49]

Substantially, in fact, the *2011 Guidelines* mostly consolidate previous case-law. If on the one hand they are designed to help undertakings determine whether their co-operation agreements are compatible with the revised competition rules by providing the above-discussed criteria for assessing the application of the competition rules, on the other hand they maintain that context-specific approach that reverts on a case-by-case assessment basis, which may be considered as of limited value.[50] Overall, they do not add anything much to what it has already been discussed so far in this work.

For the financial services sector, the *2011 Guidelines* incorporate and recall the ruling in *Asnef*, after which the European Commission's position is that the exchange of consumer data in markets with asymmetric information may generate efficiencies.

Clearly, in the financial services sector the perspective is that of asymmetries from the side of the industry, where lenders do not know as much as their customers do about their finances and their ability or willingness to perform the contract. It is not a perspective of asymmetries from the viewpoint of the customers and the efficiencies so created. This latter perspective is the usual information paradigm that needs correction in market theory to rebalance the knowledge of consumers of the supply-side of the market in order to make correct choices, as well as their contractual power. As explicated in Chap. 2, here the position is that keeping track of the past behaviour of customers provides them with an incentive to limit the exposure to risks, also allowing the detection by the industry of those customers who carry lower risks and should deserve lower prices.[51]

This view, which is consistent with the reviewed economic theory, hardly seems to consider the reciprocal influence of the market behaviour of competitors but it can also be criticised on a greater number of points. The critiques will become clearer in the Sections and Chapters below of this work.

---

[48] European Commission's Notice concerning agreements, decisions and concerted practices in the field of co-operation between enterprises, OJ 1968, C 75/3, replaced by the Commission's Guidelines on the applicability of Article 81 to horizontal co-operation agreements, OJ 2001, C 3/2, in turn replaced by the Commission's Guidelines on the applicability of Article 101 of the Treaty on the Functioning of the European Union to horizontal co-operation agreements, *supra* note 45.

[49] von Papp (forthcoming). Seitz (2011), pp. 452–462. *Contra* see Camesasca et al. (2010), pp. 405–417.

[50] See, for example, von Papp (forthcoming) who nevertheless defends the *2011 Guidelines* for being based on sound antitrust policy and reflecting existing case-law. The weakness of remaining vague is attributed as a necessary consequence of the broad range of information exchanges covered.

[51] European Commission, in OECD (2010), sp. 319.

In addition, however, the European Commission standpoint embraces the competitive element of the reduction of consumer lock-in in their relationship with financial institutions. As information is specific to a relationship with one lender, consumers would risk losing the benefit from this information for or when switching to another financial institution.[52]

Again, this assessment is not exempt from controversy. The competitive value of market intelligence of undertakings is diminished, and there is an underlying assumptions that consumers are unable to provide the information themselves and/ or they may be mistrusted. Most of all, the whole position relies on logics imposed by the financial industry where the risk of losing what is assigned as a benefit becomes an asset, and where the other side of the coin is not considered, i.e. that the labelling of a consumer by one market player—be it positive or negative— determines the fate of the switching with other competitors.

Also, this position underestimates the possibility of data portability by the consumers themselves, which inter alia in the future will be granted by law.[53]

This kind of considerations will be the subject matter of the following sections.

3.5 A Caveat: Scope of Application

In view of the positions expressed by the CJEU and the European Commission, before engaging in any comment or analysis it becomes important to ascertain what type of information is involved and whether all information could be indistinctly exchanged. This matter may be tricky for the variety of type and form of information exchanged at national level within the Member States.

Asnef clearly deals with the exchange of negative data, i.e. the exchange of information with a negative connotation on the payment history and financial behaviour of consumers, such as defaults on payments, delays, delinquencies, bankruptcies, or insolvencies.[54]

By contrast, it does not refer to the exchange of positive data about the financial standing, payments, and other details that do not indicate a default or late payment, which is not allowed in Spain. This is important as the whole reasoning of the CJEU is premised on the efficiency gains of the removal of the uncertainty of the solvency of customers and risk assessment to favour competition.

Likewise, the European Commission is clear in making reference to 'accidents or credit defaults' of consumers when keeping track of their past behaviour for pro-competitive efficiencies.

---

[52] Ibid.

[53] Proposal for a Regulation of the European Parliament and of the Council on the protection of individuals with regard to the processing of personal data and on the free movement of such data (General Data Protection Regulation), COM (2012) 11 final of 25/1/2012.

[54] *Asnef*, para 7. In Spain only registries with negative data are allowed.

This feature is corroborated by the requisite of 'indispensability' of Article 101 TFEU which makes reference to what is strictly necessary to achieve said efficiency gains generated by an information exchange.[55]

The express reference to the assessment of the risk of default/creditworthiness of consumers to favour competition rules out the automatic compliance or compatibility with the decision of information exchanges of positive financial data or exchanges of non-credit data alongside negative credit data, such as data on telecoms, utilities, mail orders, etc., whose relevance for the predictability of risk or default is undemonstrated, or at least controversial or not used in a number of Member States, including Spain. Indeed, as shown above in this work, different models of exchanging consumer financial information exist within the EU, a number of which do not make use of positive or other data regardless of the institutional form that they take. Such diversity and the impossibility of determining which system works better or is necessary, alongside the indeterminacy of where in the Member States financial institutions better assess risk and consumers suffer less problems of over-indebtedness, all make any assessment unworkable. In any case, positive or non-credit data would be capable of affecting different economic spheres of consumers and their sharing remains questionable.[56]

The problem is that in many jurisdictions credit bureaus, especially the commercial ones, exchange indistinctively both positive and negative data, with some like in the UK including non-credit data.

As the sharing of positive and non-credit data falls outside the scope of the exempted exchanges, does it make them anti-competitive?

Many arguments could be raised that falling outside the scope of application of the ruling and for all it has been written so far they pose a problem under Article 101 TFEU. By contrast, the credit data industry would argue the opposite and it will put the excluded data on the same level as the negative ones, possibly lobbying for the inclusion of others.

The reality is that this is not a trivial matter but it has remained without an answer and finds no guidance, leaving that thick veil of uncertainty that is so detrimental for a legal system.

At any rate, regardless of the distinction between positive and negative data, the type and sources of data shared also differ from Member State to Member State, which also leaves open the question as to what information can be legitimately shared in order to avoid strategic but anti-competitive purposes rather than those related to credit risk reduction as pinpointed by the CJEU.

The lack of understanding of the type of data 'necessary' for the purpose and the diverse practices from Member State to Member State make it impossible to ascertain which exchange has to be considered legitimate and which one is not.

Similarly, the degree of detail of the information to be exchanged differently used in the Member States—i.e. whether in a detailed form with all the particulars

---

[55] See Article 101(3) TFEU and the *2011 Guidelines*, *cit. supra* at 45, para 101.

[56] These issues have been tackled in Ferretti (2008, 2010), pp. 1–27.

of the history of the credit lines or in a consolidated form—make it impossible to set a general standard for legitimacy. As noted, if anything, *Asnef* confirms that information in an aggregate, consolidated form poses fewer problems for competition purposes, which is arguably the type of exchange less practiced within the EU where commercial credit bureaus outnumber the public ones.

Certainly, not all sharing in the widest sense could be permissible.

Again, the problem is that the diversity that exists from Member State to Member State renders any such assessment unworkable.

But *Asnef* does not address what information is needed, and this remains critical not only for possible risk reduction but also for competition law purposes.

What most would agree that it is certain is that in the silence of the judiciary and in the absence of guidelines, this is not something that should be left to the unilateral determination and interpretation of the financial services industry.

3.6 A Critique: Economic and Juridical Assumptions, and Remaining Uncertainty

The theory surrounding the exchange of consumer information by private entities is not free from controversy. Ignoring *tout court* behavioural economics, it is premised on economic assumptions that look at past behaviour as being predictive of future behaviour, as well as repayment behaviour of consumers as reputation collateral for their future behaviour. These economic assumptions find no justification in a relationship of cause and effect.

Likewise, despite limited but undemonstrated claims to the contrary,[57] there is no conclusive or empirical evidence that support such economic theories. On the contrary, failure to repay debts by consumers has been found to be mostly grounded on life-time events such as poor macro-economic conditions, job losses, illness or family deaths, separation and divorce, etc. that cannot be predicted with credit histories and could penalise consumers even further if used as reputation collateral.[58]

Unfortunately, the CJEU does not seem to be interested in investigating the debatable nature of these economic premises but it endorses them uncritically.[59] By contrast, consumer associations have widely voiced concerns about the ability of credit data to adequately reflect individual situations as well as how the data are assessed.[60] Moreover, in so doing, the CJEU and the European Commission

---

[57] The World Bank (2011), Jappelli and Pagano (1999).

[58] Ramsay (2007), sp. 578–580; Caplovitz (1963), Adler and Wozniak (1980), Berthoud and Kempson (1992), Hoermann (1986), Elliott (2005), Balmer et al. (2006), pp. 39–51; Dominy and Kempson (2003).

[59] *Asnef*, para 47.

[60] European Commission (2009).

confuse, or omit to consider, the models of those Member States where private or commercial registries do not exist, such as those where the absence of such bureaus does not prevent them to be on the same footing with other Member States in terms of credit provision or likelihood of debt repayment by consumers. For example, no evidence suggests that Belgium or France are problematic jurisdictions in terms of household over-indebtedness and/or default rates compared with the Netherlands, Italy or the UK.[61]

In this context, it is worth repeating how critical it is the distinction between public and private credit bureaus. This, in fact, seems to represent the fundamental misconception of the CJEU capable of affecting subsequently its judgement. The Court premises its judgement on the postulation that "the information contained in the register is similar to *that provided for in Circular 3/1995, which regulates the Central de Informacion de Riesgos (...) operated by the Spanish central bank*"[62] *[emphasis added]*. However, as noted previously, public and private registers serve different economic and institutional purposes, where the former are managed and designed under precise rules that follow a proper regulatory path.

Likewise, the CJEU suggests that "the *necessary participation* of the credit institutions in that register *inevitably* entails a certain amount of cooperation between competitors in the form of an indirect exchange of credit information"[63] [emphasis added], thus making applicable Article 101 TFEU and excluding from the outset "any need to characterise precisely the *form of the cooperation* thus established between those institutions"[64] [emphasis added].

As seen above, however, one of the distinguishing features of private or commercial credit bureaus is the voluntary and contractual nature of the relationship between the latter and the participating lenders. Quite the opposite, if anything, the private contractual nature of the relationship may represent a problem in terms of bank competition. Previous studies have pointed out how the use of these credit bureaus can be used for the strategic foreclosure of existing and new market entrants, especially in the case of large banks which may have the incentive not to disclose their complete portfolio of borrowers in terms of either comprehensiveness or accuracy of information to deter others from benefiting from it.[65]

This behaviour is only possible in a voluntary, contract-based system.

---

[61] A comparison between the UK and France suggests rather the opposite. See Ramsay (2012), pp. 212–248.

[62] *Asnef*, para 7.

[63] Ibid., para. 30.

[64] Ibid., para 31.

[65] European Commission "Report on the retail banking sector inquiry" Commission Staff Working Document accompanying the Communication from the Commission—Sector Inquiry under Art 17 of Regulation 1/2003 on retail banking (Final Report) [COM(2007) 33 final] SEC(2007) 106. See also Bouckaert and Degryse (2004), pp. 27–52; Bouckaert and Degryse (2006), pp. 702–720; Gehrig and Stenbacka (2007), pp. 77–99; Giannetti et al. (2010).

Public bureaus, by contrast, would sanction it with fines or suspension/withdrawal of licenses, a power that commercial entities do not and cannot have.[66] This is a market behaviour backed by evidence in the US where large-scale omissions and incomplete credit reports have been exposed through the use of private credit bureaus.[67]

Besides, the related CJEU assertions that the examined bureau "is in principle open to any institution active in the sphere of loans and credit"[68] and therefore "appear capable of having an appreciable significance in the choice of undertakings established in Member States other than the Kingdom of Spain as to whether or not to do business in that State"[69] appear frail and unrealistic claims. The volume-based fee structure applied by credit bureaus for the supply of information (information cannot be sold one by one) and the information reciprocity requirements in place (to be part of the system lending institutions have to supply information otherwise the other participants would not supply information in first place and the system would be inaccurate) are seen as elements likely to be a barrier for new market entrants (that do not have information to supply) or smaller lenders (that supply less information than larger ones), thus restraining competition.[70]

Last but not least, by referring to the 'necessary' participation in a voluntary system or by emphasising its criticality to avoid anti-competitive adverse selection problems, it is unclear whether it suggests a *de facto* obligation for lenders to contract with private or commercial credit bureaus. This not only would clearly be an ossimoron. Assuming that the system is as beneficial as the CJEU suggests, may any market player allow himself not to participate in it? Would they be forced as a matter of fact to contract with national private credit bureaus to remain competitive?

True, the CJEU claims that "such systems (...) are not liable to reduce uncertainty as to the risks of competition" and "each operator could be expected to act independently and autonomously when adopting a given course of conduct, regard being had to the risks presented by applicants".[71] However, within the same market segment, in practice it may be difficult for a lender to depart from the course of action taken by a competitor (e.g. a rejection) since a claimed principal benefit of the system is to avoid that information asymmetry could lead to adverse selection where a lender attracts those consumers who were previously rejected by others.

---

[66] See also Giannetti et al. (2010).

[67] Avery et al. (2004).

[68] *Asnef*, para 41.

[69] *Asnef*, para 42.

[70] European Commission "Report on the retail banking sector inquiry" Commission Staff Working Document accompanying the Communication from the Commission—Sector Inquiry under Art 17 of Regulation 1/2003 on retail banking (Final Report) [COM(2007) 33 final] SEC(2007) 106.

[71] *Asnef*, para 62.

At any rate, as the focus is on the conduct to be taken with regard to the risks presented by applicants, it would be a source of concern if in so reasoning the CJEU accepted and legitimised the classification or sorting of consumers, where operators are entitled to divide people in economic segments in which they are expected to act independently and autonomously by specialising in the market segment of choice, but at the same time being reciprocally influenced within the same segment. This interpretation would also support the practice of economic sorting which, in the area of financial services for consumers, may easily translate in social sorting and impact on the social sphere of individuals. If this view has to be rejected, it remains the conundrum relating to the relationship between the 'necessity' of participation in a voluntary information exchange system, independent and autonomous behaviour in market segmentation, and expected behaviour within market segments in theory and in practice.

All the above is compounded by the consideration that the CJEU reasoning assumes accuracy of the information exchanged, where accuracy is intertwined with universal coverage and participation. In fact, an incomplete system, or a system where not all market participants adhere, is inaccurate by definition precisely for the information that is not there. At the same time, the concept of a system that is voluntary and governed by private law (contract), and at the same time requires to be universal in participation and coverage is a *contradictio in terminis*, if not *in adiecto*.

An additional point to consider is that information exchanged in a voluntary system is not verified or vetted by a third party but it relies on the unilateral determination of those who provide it, a circumstance which not only poses challenges to the authority of such information to determine who is and who is not creditworthy, but ultimately it impinges on accuracy.

The problem is that under the same determination of the CJEU, reproduced in the *2011 Guidelines*, compatibility with EU competition law cannot be assessed in the abstract but it depends on the economic conditions of the relevant markets and on specific characteristics of the system concerned which include, among the others, comprehensiveness and accuracy. How can information exchange in voluntary private credit bureaus be compatible with EU competition law if the system cannot be accurate unless participation is mandated to all market players and information vetted? Are not these the features previously identified as owing to those bureaus that are public institutions?

In the end, once more failure to distinguish between private and public credit registries turns out to become critical, with important implications for competition law and policy. This is compounded by the findings of the only existing empirical research on the effects of credit registries on banking market concentration and on competition indicators, which concluded that only public registries increase market entries, have a significant negative effect on market concentration and contribute to the intensification of competition. Private credit bureaus, by contrast, were not found to show significant effects on market structure. The study ultimately recommends that countries that would like to strengthen competition in financial services could consider setting up a public credit register, which—as seen—are also a valuable tool for financial stability and prudential supervision of financial institutions.[72]

Moreover, from the perspective of competition, public bureaus have the safeguard of sharing aggregate data, a feature that cannot be found in the processing of data by private bureaus and that remains open to challenge in the case-by-case assessment as determined by the CJEU.

A final consideration appears important. On the one hand the CJEU rules that the information exchange of credit bureaus is in principle permissible if relevant markets are not highly concentrated.[73] On the other hand this determination clashes with the reality of markets in retail financial services in the EU. The latest sector inquiry of the Commission reports that several markets in the EU suffer from high concentration levels.[74] Such findings, if applied to the CJEU ruling, would probably outlaw the majority of information exchanges by credit bureaus, unless the third limb of Article 101 TFEU is applied and the concentration allows consumers a fair share of the benefit.

This will be looked at later in Chap. 5.

3.7 Concluding Remarks

Competition policy, law, and enforcement have become an established feature of historically protected financial services markets, especially in the context of the integration of the EU financial market. The exchange of commercially sensitive information among competitors is a traditional grey area in the enforcement of EU competition law. Information exchanges may be pro- or anti-competitive depending on a number of elements to be assessed on a case-by-case basis. The case law of the CJEU and policy documents of the competent European authorities provide some general guidance but they confirm the difficulties and uncertainties inherent in a determination that must be established without general and theoretical rules to distinguish between a legitimate and an illegitimate information exchange and the analysis of specific economic contexts and, in case of anti-competitive agreements or practices, the possible predominant positive effect for consumers.

In the retail financial sector the CJEU has intervened with the decision in *Asnef*, providing some clarity and certainty in the sector. Likewise, the European Commission has retrieved the decision of the Court in its guidelines.

---

[72] Giannetti et al. (2010).

[73] See *Asnef* and the *Guidelines*.

[74] European Commission "Report on the retail banking sector inquiry" Commission Staff Working Document accompanying the Communication from the Commission—Sector Inquiry under Art 17 of Regulation 1/2003 on retail banking (Final Report) [COM(2007) 33 final] SEC(2007) 106.

Nonetheless, a number of obscure elements remain, starting from the type of information considered by the European authorities, which are only the negative ones and leave out the exchange of positive data. The problem is that in many Member States also positive and other information is exchanged, leaving uncertainty as to the legitimacy of such practices.

In addition, the reliance on economic and juridical assumptions alongside other unclear elements regarding participation in a system that is voluntary and problems of accuracy, coupled with the different legal nature and purposes for exchanging information that occur in the different Member States, leave in place undesirable uncertainties and scope for criticisms.

The impression is that several aspects of how and why information is exchanged are omitted, neglected, confused or blurred.

These may not be secondary aspects and, in general, they cast doubts over the righteousness or justice of the position taken.

Most and foremost, however, by concentrating exclusively on the competition side of financial institutions but leaving out any determination as to the underlying information market, the position taken appears unsatisfactory and it may be challenged also as regards the integration of EU retail financial markets and competition in the market of information itself. These latter aspects will be covered in the following Chapter.

References

Adler M, Wozniak E (1980) The origins and consequences of default—an examination of the impact of diligence. Research Report n. 6, Scottish Law Commission

Almunia J (2012) New rules for finance: putting the genie back in the bottle. SPEECH/12/648 (24 September 2012). http://europa.eu/rapid/press-release_SPEECH-12-648_en.htm

Avery RP, Calem P, Canner G (2004) Credit report accuracy and access to credit, federal reserve bulletin. Summer, Washington

Balmer N, Pleasence P, Buck A, Walker H (2006) Worried sick: the experience of debt problems and their relationship with health, illness and disability. Soc Policy Soc 5(1):39–51

Beck T, Demirguc-Kunt A, Levine R (2006) Bank concentration, competition and crises. J Bank Finan 30:1581–1603

Beitel P, Schiereck D, Wahrenburg M (2004) Explaining M&A success in European banks. Eur Finan Manag 10:109–140

Bennett M, Collins P (2010) The law and economics of information sharing: the good, the bad, and the ugly. Eur Competition J 6:311–337

Berger A, Klapper LF, Turk-Ariss R (2009) Bank competition and financial stability. J Finan Serv Res 35:99–118

Berthoud R, Kempson E (1992) Credit and debt: The PSI report. PSI

Bouckaert JH, Degryse H (2006) Entry and strategic information display in credit markets. Econ J 116:702–720

Bouckaert JH, Degryse H (2004) Softening competition by inducing switching in credit markets. J Ind Econ 52:27–52

Boutler L (1999) Competition risks in benchmarking. Eur Competition Law Rev 20:434–441

Camesasca PD, Schmidt AK, Clancy MJ (2010) The EC commission's draft horizontal guidelines: presumed guilty when having a chat. J Eur Competition Law Pract 1(5):405–417

Caplovitz D (1963) The poor pay more: consumer practices of low income families. Free Press, New York

Capobianco A (2004) Information exchange under EC competition law. Common Mark Law Rev 41:1247–1276

Carle J, Johnsson M (1998) Benchmarking and EC competition law. Eur Competition Law Rev 19(2):74–84

Carletti E, Vives X (2009) Regulation and competition policy in the banking sector. In Vives X (ed) Fifty years of the treaty of Rome: assessment and perspectives of competition policy in Europe. Oxford University Press, Oxford

Carletti E, Vives X (2008) Regulation and competition in the banking sector. Occasional Paper no. OP-159 IESE Business School, University of Navarra

Carletti E (2009) Competition and regulation in banking. In: Thakor A, Boot A (eds) Handbook of financial intermediation and banking. Elsevier, London, pp 449–482

Clarke RN (1983) Collusion and the incentives for information sharing. Bell J Econ 14:383–394

Dermine J (2003) European banking: past, present, and future. In: Gaspar V, Hartmann P, Sleijpen O (eds) The transformation of the European financial system. European Central Bank, Frankfurt, pp 31–95

Dominy N, Kempson E (2003) Can't pay or won't pay? a review of creditor and debtor approaches to the non-payment of bills. DCA, London

Elliott A (2005) Not waving but drowning: over-indebtedness by misjudgment. CSFI, New York

Ferretti F (2010) A European perspective on consumer loans and the role of credit registries: the need to reconcile data protection, risk management, efficiency, over-indebtedness, and a better prudential supervision of the financial system. J Consum Policy 33(1):1–27

Ferretti F (2008) The law and consumer credit information systems in the EC. Routledge-Cavendish, London

Franchoo T, Beaten N, Cranley S (2012) The application of European competition law in the financial services sector. J Eur Competition Law Pract 4(4):345–364

Gehrig T, Stenbacka R (2007) Information sharing and lending market competition with switching costs and poaching. Eur Econ Rev 51:77–99

Giannetti C, Jentzsch N, Spagnolo G (2010) Information-sharing and cross-border entry in European banking. ECRI Research Report N. 11, Brussels

Henry BR (1994) Benchmarking and antitrust. Antitrust Law J 62:483–512

Hoermann G (ed) (1986) Consumer credit and consumer insolvency: perspectives for legal policy from Europe and the USA. ZERP, Bremen

Jappelli T, Pagano M (1999) Information sharing, lending and default: cross-country evidence. CSEF working paper No. 22. Salerno, University of Salerno, Italy

Lista A (2013) EU competition law and the financial services sector. Informa· Law from Routledge, London

Meyring B (2009) T-Mobile: Further confusion on information exchanges between competitors: Case C-8, 08 T-Mobile Netherlands and others, ECR 0000. J European Competition Law Pract 1(1):30–32

Monti G (2007) EC competition law. Cambridge University Press, Cambridge

OECD (2010) Policy round tables: information exchanges between competitors under competition law. DAF/COMP 37

Ortega Gonzalez A (2012) Object analysis in information exchange among competitors. Glob Antitrust Rev 5:1–57

Posner RA (1979) Information and antitrust: reflections on the gypsum and engineers decisions. Georgetown Law J 67:1187–1203

Ramsay I (2012) A tale of two debtors: responding to the shock of over-indebtedness in France and England—a story from the Trente Piteuses. Mod Law Rev 75:212–248

Ramsay I (2007) Consumer law and policy. Hart, Oxford

Scherer FM, Ross D (1990) Industrial market structure and economic performance. Houghton Mifflin, Boston

Seitz C (2011) One step in the right direction—the new horizontal guidelines and the restated block exemption regulations. J Eur Competition Law Pract 2(5):452–462

The World Bank (2011) General principles for credit reporting. Washington

Van den Bergh RJ, Camesasca PD (2006) European competition law and economics: a comparative perspective. Thomson Sweet and Maxwell, London

Van Tassel E, Vishwasrao S (2007) Asymmetric information and the mode of entry in foreign credit markets. J Bank Finan 31:3742–3760

Vives X (2006) Information sharing, economics and anti-trust: the pros and cons of information sharing. In: Swedish Competition Authority (ed) The pros and cons of information sharing. Stockholm, Leanders Grafiska, pp 83–100

Vives X (1991) Regulatory reform in Europe. Eur Econ Rev 35:505–515

von Papp FW (2013) Information exchange agreements. In: Geradin D, Lianos I (eds.) Research handbook on EU Antitrust Law. Edward Elgar Publishing, Forthcoming. http://www.ssrn.com/abstract=2015674. Accessed 20 June 2013

von Papp FW (2007) Who is that can inform me?—the exchange of identifying and non-identifying information. Eur Competition Law Rev 28(4):264–270

Whish R (2012) Competition law. Oxford University Press, Oxford

Whish R (2006) Information agreements. In Swedish Competition Authority (ed) The pros and cons of information sharing. Leanders Grafiska, Stockholm, pp 19–42

Chapter 4
The Integration of EU Retail Financial Markets and Competition Law in Information Markets

4.1 Introduction

In the field of competition, national competence and EU competence are autonomous and parallel, the latter being defined by the criterion of the effect of trade among Member States.[1] The CJEU remit to decide on the legitimacy of the behaviour of undertakings in the market is dictated by the actual or potential European dimension of the matter at stake, i.e. agreements, decisions or practices which may affect trade between EU countries within the meaning of Article 101 TFEU, as well as the interpretation of EU law.[2]

Moreover, as it was anticipated earlier in Chap. 3, from its origins the rationale of EU competition law was tied to the achievement of the single market goal, which still remains one of its main declared objectives. As seen earlier, the Treaty of Lisbon has reinforced the view that competition is no longer an end in itself but

---

[1] Moussis (2013).
[2] See official website of the European Union at http://europa.eu/legislation_summaries/competition/firms/l26110_en.htm "Council Regulation (EC) No 1/2003 on the implementation of the competition rules laid down in Articles 101 and 102 of the Treaty on the Functioning of the European Union (TFEU) (ex-Articles 81 and 82 of the Treaty Establishing the European Community (TEC)) establishes a system of parallel competences in which the Commission, European Union (EU) countries' competent national competition authorities and national courts can all apply Articles 101 and 102 TFEU. National courts can apply Articles 101 and 102 TFEU without it being necessary to apply national competition law in parallel. However, where a national court applies national competition law to agreements, decisions or practices which may affect trade between EU countries within the meaning of Article 101(1) TFEU (ex-Article 81(1) TEC) or to any abuse prohibited by Article 102 TFEU, they also have to apply EU competition rules to those agreements, decisions or practices".

© The Author(s) 2014
F. Ferretti, *EU Competition Law, the Consumer Interest and Data Protection*,
SpringerBriefs in Law, DOI 10.1007/978-3-319-08906-5_4

a means to serve the internal market and its integration, thus reorienting competition policy towards consistency with other EU policies and activities.[3]

As far as market integration is concerned, until the 1970s banking and financial services activities in the Member States were heavily regulated at a national level and they remained a national business. For instance, controls were in place both on interest rates and credit growth as part of an anti-inflationary policy based on the control of money supply.[4]

Since the beginning of the 1980s, however, the regulatory framework governing consumer finance has undergone a deep transformation both at national and at Community level. Financial sector reforms included the liberalisation of cross-country capital flows and the deregulation of domestic capital markets, ultimately having the scope to liberalise the provision of financial services and to increase competition. The removal of capital movement restrictions, the establishment of a harmonised framework for financial services, and the enactment of a directive for consumer credit ('CCD')[5] all seemed steps towards an integrated credit market.[6] The recently passed mortgage credit directive ('MCD')[7] aims to reinforce integration further.

Yet, today the reality of European markets in consumer finance presents a picture different from the envisaged one.

Extensive economic research demonstrates that markets are still far from being integrated. This conclusion is derived from the existence of a number of barriers among the Member States, as well as several integration indicators such as real price and interest differentials, absence of cross-border lending, poor market penetration by foreign lenders, the existence of large differences from country to country in the extension of consumer loans, differentials in demand, business models, language, and consumers' cultural and psychological factors in the use of credit.[8]

As a result of this fragmentation of the European markets in consumer finance, so far not only financial services for consumers have developed differently from one Member State to another, but they have also done so at a different pace with different organisational structures.

Thus, it is not surprising that these differences are transposed in the consumer financial data industry, which has mirrored the development of the underlying financial markets and has concentrated domestically, neglecting either a European dimension or the cross-border exchange of data.

---

[3] Graham (2010), Whish (2012). See also Chap. 3 and the relevant literature cited.

[4] Lista (2013), Carletti and Vives (2009).

[5] Directive 2008/48/EC of the European Parliament and of the Council of 23 April 2008 on credit agreements for consumers and repealing Council Directive 87/102/EEC, OJ 2008 L 133/66.

[6] Diez Guardia (2002), Wyman (2005).

[7] Directive 2014/17/EU of the European Parliament and of the Council of 4 February 2014 on credit agreements for consumers relating to residential immovable property and amending Directives 2008/48/EC and 2013/36/EU and Regulation (EU) No 1093/2010, OJ 2014 L 60/34.

[8] Wyman (2005), Riestra (2002), p. 5; Jentzsch and San José Riestra (2003), p. 8; Jentzsch and San José Riestra (2006), pp. 27–62; Weill (2004), sp. 3–6; Crook (2003), Guiso (2003), Lea et al. (1995), pp. 681–701; Diez Guardia (2002), p. 7; Lanoo and de la Mata Muñoz (2004), sp. 3–4; Buch (2000).

Alongside this uneven development of retail finance, however, the information distribution industry—or information market—presents peculiarities of its own in relation to the industrial organisation and the institutional structure serving the markets, described earlier in Chap. 2. The latter, for example, translates in the division between the different legal or institutional form of private and public credit bureaus, that pursue different objectives in the Member States. As a consequence, regulatory barriers at national level exist to the extent that public credit bureaus are subjected to regulatory frameworks to perform their different functions in the economy. As seen earlier, these barriers may extend to when access to credit bureaus by lenders is restricted by the kind of activity that an institution must conduct, the condition of holding certain licenses, and their submission to the rules of the systems, including penalties and obligations beyond contract.

As far as market integration is concerned, information markets have a twofold feature.

On the one side, an exchange of information among competitors at EU level may have defined pro-competitive effects. On the other side, however, it may present at various levels additional barriers to market integration in its own right, which in turn have a direct impact on the underlying market in consumer finance that they serve.

Therefore, if on the one hand it is true that the fragmented information market originates from the fragmentation of the underlying retail financial market, on the other hand its features and infrastructure may in turn constitute a barrier for the changes put forward by the EU legislator to enhance the integration of retail financial markets. The argument is that in intertwined markets reforms in one market may be compromised or frustrated if the other market is unaffected by the same reforms and remains fragmented.

Arguably, therefore, the fragmented market structure in the consumer financial data industry pictured in Chap. 3 plays an important part in the poor exchange of information among European consumer credit bureaus. This leads to the consideration that to date the EU still has an underdeveloped information structure.

At the same time, a possible exchange of information among European credit bureaus would open debates over the competitive nature of the data industry, for example in terms of legitimacy of partitioning of the EU market into national markets and exchanging information among themselves without competing, or at the opposite side of the spectrum even in terms of competition in an open EU market for information. After all, it should not be forgotten that the legal form of most credit bureaus is that of commercial companies incorporated as any other company in the marketplace.

Alternatively, and to the extent that other defined policy objectives are considered dominant, it could be imagined an European information exchange system among public institutions at national level or, why not, a central European database under the control of a public authority such as the European Central Bank or any other institution with supervisory powers and in control of the levels of indebtedness in the EU.

Probably these considerations go too far in the imagination or they may be visionary. In any event, what remains important is to assess to what extent the current arrangements for the exchange of information really enhances competition, they open national markets, and thus they foster integration in the EU. Under this perspective, not only the retail financial sector should be looked at but also the information market should be considered.

4.2 Market Integration and Pro-competitive Effects of Information Exchanges

4.2.1 Establishment of Competitors in Another Member State

The exchange of consumer financial information may have pro-competitive effects for market integration in the establishment of a physical commercial presence of a financial institution in another EU jurisdiction.

As seen in Chap. 3, *Asnef* and the *2011 Guidelines* have attempted to provide a clarification from a competition law perspective of the conditions in which financial institutions may engage in an information exchange. This represented a much needed effort to shed light on a traditionally controversial area of law. Under this perspective, efforts to remove uncertainty and guide national competition authorities towards a common approach in the EU are positive per se.

From the perspective of the financial industry and the establishment of the EU market, information exchanges may have an encouraging effect on certain types of market entry mode of new or foreign lenders in another Member State. In particular, this may be the case in the establishment of a physical presence of a financial institution in another jurisdiction.

An increase in the number of cross-border mergers and acquisitions is often seen as an indicator of more integrated markets.[9] Foreign lenders who acquire or merge with an existing local market player could benefit from the latter pre-existing participation in an information exchange system. Similarly, as made clear by the CJEU—and provided for in the CCD and in the MCD—newly set-up institutions or institutions that establish a branch in another Member State shall not be discriminated in the participation in such a system. This is at least in law, where the CJEU decision provides for the guarantee of accessibility to all operators in order not to be placed at disadvantage for the purpose of risk assessment.[10]

Looking at the issue of non-discrimination in practice, however, this may be more complex by the requirement of reciprocity inherent in the information

---

[9] Giannetti et al. (2010).

[10] *Asnef*, para 60.

exchange systems: those who want to participate and receive information need necessarily provide information.

The problem is that credit bureaus are national systems and usually the condition for participation is the supply of lenders' data portfolio. This reciprocity principle is the bloodline of any information exchange system. Reciprocity is theoretically possible but it may be hard to meet, if not impossible, for new institutions or foreign lenders which do not have a national portfolio of data. Existing participants to what is a voluntary system, and who are at the same time the clients of private or commercial credit bureaus and pay for their services, may be reluctant to share their portfolio of data with competitors in return for nothing, or later data only once the new competing businesses develop and gain a share of the market. Not surprisingly, some economic literature reports that participants to a voluntary information exchange system are traditionally adverse to free-riders in the system.[11]

In the end, therefore, under this standpoint the CJEU decision and the *2011 Guidelines* may serve the purpose of competition forcing existing market players not to obstruct newcomers, not only in law but also in fact, giving to the latter legal tools for enforcement.

As such, they should be applauded. Rather, the question could be whether credit bureaus in a voluntary system will be forced to contract with them, undermining basic principles of contract law and freedom of contract. This is, however, a matter rooted in and deeply affecting commercial law and it is for further research to explore separately.

At any rate, if on the one hand clarity and pro-market entry of foreign lenders represent helpful steps and shed some light in view of an EU competitive market integration, on the other hand the position taken by the CJEU and the European Commission raise a number of questions which nurture concerns on a number of several other accounts which this work aims to investigate further.

4.3 Cross-Border Services, Competition, and Non-Discrimination

4.3.1 Cross-Border Provision or Receipt of Services

The previous Section has acknowledged the encouraging effect of sharing consumer information for market entry in other jurisdictions and competition, which entails a commercial presence in a Member State, and which is one aspect of EU financial market integration in the retail sector.

However, unfair or discriminatory access conditions for foreign lenders may take place in circumstances different from the establishment of a physical presence

---

[11] Giannetti et al. (2010).

in a Member State. At EU level there are other emerging modes of providing credit which are necessary for market integration. As seen earlier, *Asnef* did not address them; it made clear reference to 'the relevant market', which should not be concentrated, but in so doing it limited its vision to the national market, in that particular instance the Spanish one.

Other possible forms of market integration in the sector are the cross-border provision of services, including internet banking or e-commerce, where lenders are based in one Member State and do business with consumers in another Member State. In principle, however, under the current system non-established financial institutions do not have access to all existing credit bureaus in the EU and they would not be able to provide information to all of them any time they establish a financial relationship with a consumer.

This is because lenders from a Member State are unlikely to have or establish an ongoing contractual relationship with a private or commercial credit bureau in another Member State.

Moreover, the business model of reciprocity would prove hard to satisfy, where foreign lenders would be in the impractical situation to provide their data portfolio to the credit bureau of another country, in addition in the type and breath of data required by such a different system. Financial institutions may also be reluctant for commercial reasons re-conducible to competition matters.

At the same time, in a commercial environment, the existing national participants may be averse to share their data portfolios with foreign players and allow competition on their market from abroad on a basis that is not reciprocal.

Likewise, in the case of public credit bureaus, foreign lenders do not have to abide by the national rules of another Member State if not physically established there (provided they qualify as 'banks').

The described complex scenario may have practical implications.

The following example may illustrate some of the issues at stake.

Let's suppose UK lender 'A' granting a loan to UK consumer 'John'. Lender A checks UK credit bureau(s) and supplies back to it the information it generates once concluding or denying the contract with John. Lender A already shares its portfolio of data on a reciprocal basis via the UK bureau. Now suppose that John applies for a loan to lender 'B' cross-border in Italy. Lender B would need access to the UK credit bureau(s), but it is not a member. As it will be seen below in greater detail, in theory Lender B would now be able to access the UK credit bureau(s), albeit with practical difficulties, and furnish back information. The information would only be that of the specific credit line with John. At the same time, the data on that same credit line would not be provided to the Italian credit bureau. Even more unlikely, the same data will not feed the credit bureaus of all other Member States for future financial activities that John may engage in, e.g. buying goods at favourable instalment prices on the internet. All in all, Lender B will not disclose all of its existing portfolio of data to other foreign bureaus.

The situation may increasingly complicate if we take as example a French resident entering into negotiation cross-border with a foreign lender. By law, France does not allow the operation of commercial credit bureaus and requires on banks the compulsory reporting to the *Banque de France* with its own rules. Now the French Constitutional Court has declared positive information in credit bureaus unconstitutional,[12] which makes their availability impossible for foreign lenders that usually require them in their home Member State.

These are purely imaginary scenarios which may even work in theory, provided that credit bureaus supply the type, amount, and level of coverage of information required by lenders of other Member States and lenders are able to provide back only that information compatible with the foreign system. In few words, the regulation and harmonisation of information systems and their legal form may fix the conundrum.

Possibly, this kind of market organisation may be opposed with the argument that the whole issue is a nicety because there is a lack of demand or supply for cross-border lending to retail customers, or that there is no evidence that this is needed for market integration given the negligible appetite for and volume of this type of market. However, if the limited cross-border lending to consumers has been used as a justification for not intervening in the corresponding information market, it is now undisputed that the restrictions to cross-border exchanges of information are a major factor for this limited provision of services.[13]

In any case, it is the task of the EU to create the level playing field to make it possible in a single market, stimulating such type of market activity and then leaving it to the market to determine if and to what extent this type of financial activities may take-off. But this may occur only once the level playing field exists. To create such conditions and open the markets, competition policy and law may play an important role.

4.3.2 The EU Directives: Consumer Credit and Mortgage Loans

From this perspective, legal measures have already intervened at EU level. However, they are only concerned with the market of lenders, but not with that of the information industry.

The CCD—in its unclear provision regarding the consultation of databases 'where necessary' as opposed to obtaining information directly from consumers 'where appropriate'[14]—already requires that in the case of cross-border credit Member States have to ensure access for creditors from other Member States to databases used in that Member State for assessing the creditworthiness of consumers on a non-discriminatory basis. Literally, Article 9 of the CCD provides that

---

[12] Conseil Constitutionnel, Décision n. 2014-690 DC du 13 mars 2014.

[13] This circumstance is supported by studies led and/or financed by the industry. See e.g. European Commission (2009), CEPS-ECRI (2013).

[14] Article 8 of the Consumer Credit Directive (CCD), cit. supra at note n. 4.

Each Member State shall in the case of cross-border credit ensure access for creditors from other Member States to databases used in that Member State for assessing the credit-worthiness of consumers. The conditions for access shall be non-discriminatory.[15]

Similarly, the final text of the MCD provides for an obligation for lenders to assess the consumer's creditworthiness before granting a loan. As information contained in credit bureaus is one of the tools for creditors to assess consumers' creditworthiness, the directive also contains provisions to enable non-discrimina-tory access of creditors to relevant credit databases in the creditworthiness assessment process.[16] Non-discriminatory access applies both to credit databases operated by private credit bureaus and to the public ones.[17]

The focus on competition of the MCD is clear from the Recitals:

to prevent any distortion of competition among creditors, it should be ensured that all creditors, including credit institutions or non-credit institutions providing credit agree-ments relating to residential immovable property, have access to all public and private credit databases concerning consumers under non–discriminatory conditions. Such con-ditions should not therefore include a requirement for creditors to be established as a credit institution. Access conditions, such as the costs of accessing the database or requirements to provide information to the database on the basis of reciprocity should continue to apply. Member States should be free to determine whether, within their jurisdictions, credit intermediaries may have access to such databases.[18]

While the above provisions tackle possible competition problems arising from the holding of licences, or access to private as opposed to public bureaus, con-tractual barriers relating to the compliance with reciprocity or fee structures—such as joining fees, membership fees and transaction fees—persist. The credit bureaus stipulate a range of criteria which their members, or clients, need to meet. As seen, this is either to meet public policy objectives or for the commercial companies to be profitable on volumes (one single piece of information could not be priced or profitable). These criteria are disparate across the EU. Crucially, nevertheless, reciprocity remains the key for their operation. But fee setting and reciprocity may well continue to foreclose entry or restrict competition.[19] However, they remain the pillars of the information industry, without which the business model of exchanging information through this third party agency may not exist, at least in the way it is known today.

In any event, as anticipated above, one of the main problems that persists is the depth and breadth of information in national credit bureaus which currently differ

---

[15] Ibid., Article 9.

[16] Art. 21(1) of the Mortgage Credit Directive (MCD), cit. supra at note n. 6.

[17] Ibid., Article 21(2).

[18] Ibid., Recital 60.

[19] European Commission, "Report on the retail banking sector inquiry", *Commission Staff Working Document accompanying the Communication from the Commission—Sector Inquiry under Art 17 of Regulation 1/2003 on retail banking (Final Report)* [COM(2007) 33 final] SEC(2007) 106; see also Giannetti et al. (2010).

from jurisdiction to jurisdiction, which prevent interoperability among national systems.

The depth of data makes reference to the amount of information about a credit agreement that is available.[20] The breadth of data, in turn, refers to the level of product coverage (data related to consumer credit, to mortgage credit, to not-credit related debt such as telecom or utility bills, etc.). In addition, the definitions used to assess which data should be entered into the databases also differ from a country to another. The terminologies, meanings, and significance of the data used differ substantially from Member State to Member State.

For the purpose of competition and market integration, at least to some degree greater convergence or harmonisation of credit databases should be achieved. Standardisation of certain concepts and definitions, as well as consistency in terms of the scope of data and their purpose should be achieved so as to ensure that data can be easily understood, and used fairly and objectively. The matter concerns both the underlying market in consumer finance and the market for data.

However, there remain diverging views across the Member States concerning the type of data that should be stored in credit registers. Arguably, the European Commission should take the lead in defining a common minimum set of data to be reported to the credit bureaus and made available to creditors. For the same reason and to achieve the same objectives, the legal form of credit registers should be harmonised across Member States.

In truth, at the proposal stage of the MCD the European Commission had included a provision that would have allowed to harmonise at least some key terms used in credit databases (terms such as 'defaults', 'arrears') and to define uniform credit registration criteria, as well as data processing conditions to be applied to credit databases (e.g. the registration thresholds), in order to increase reliability of information contained in databases, facilitate creditworthiness assessments and in the long-run promote cross-border supply of credit. But these provision were not kept during negotiations and in the final text of the directive.[21]

---

[20] For instance some Member States follow a comprehensive positive data reporting approach (every single credit is reported upon, independently as to whether the consumer is in arrears or not), while credit registers in other countries only engage in negative reporting (credits are only be reported upon once the consumer did not manage to meet his/her payment obligations).

[21] Commission adoption of a proposal for a Directive on credit agreements relating to residential property, COM(2011)142. The following provisions were deleted during the negotiations between the Council and the European Parliament:

Article 14(5)—"Powers are delegated to the Commission (...) to specify and amend the criteria to be considered in the conduct of a creditworthiness assessment as laid down in paragraph 1 of this Article and in ensuring that credit products are not unsuitable for the consumer as laid down in paragraph 4 of this Article".

Article 16(2)—"Powers are delegated to the Commission (...) to define uniform credit registration criteria and data processing conditions to be applied to the databases referred to in paragraph 1 of this Article. In particular, such delegated acts shall define the registration thresholds to be applied to such databases and shall provide for agreed definitions for key terms used by such databases".

As first above anticipated, this problem last identified can be re-conducted to that of absence of interoperability, which makes reference to the inability of making systems and organizations to work together (inter-operate). Currently, credit bureaus are not interoperable within the EU for a number of reasons, but mostly for the legal form of information providers, the different data and systems used, and the different criteria employed.

Failing interoperability, not only any alleged pro-competitive effects of exchanging information would vanish and market integration not achieved. But it may also pose concerns of opposite nature, that is of anti-competitive behaviour on the part of the bureaus themselves. This issue will be explored further below. Before that, and notwithstanding these problems, there is another aspect of market integration that needs to be looked at, which is tied with the other essential EU right of free movement of people.

4.4 Free Movement of People and Citizenship

4.4.1 Access to Host Member States' Services

Although the EU has clearly expressed the political drive and it has set the basis for maximum harmonisation in the sector of credit for consumers, exemplified by the CCD and the MCD, it is difficult to predict whether, when, or to what degree there will be a truly integrated European single market.

Previous studies identified the need for a European single market in consumer finance and the creation of cross-border financial opportunities as the main factors for the need of the cross-border exchange of information among information systems. According to these studies, however, the cross-border exchange of information remains hampered by an alleged reduced mobility of retail borrowers outside their own country. Therefore, banks and other financial institutions still would not have sufficient incentive to further implement such an exchange. In short, supply-demand restraints would explain the existing underdeveloped information structure in Europe.[22]

All the same, it is already apparent that for years an increasing number of people from the Member States is circulating within the EU and more are likely to follow, either in the exercise of their right of freedom of movement or freedom of establishment in another Member State.[23]

---

[22] Riestra (2002), Jentzsch and San José Riestra (2003), Jentzsch and San José Riestra (2006), pp. 27–62; Jentzsch (2003).

[23] Workers—Article 45 TFEU (ex Article 39 TEC) to Article 48 TFEU (ex Article 42 TEC). Right of Establishment—Article 49 TFEU (ex Article 43 TEC) to Article 54 TFEU (ex Article 48 TEC).

Such mobility of nationals of the Member States within the EU—together with the introduction of the Euro currency that has started to remove at least a barrier to a more open financial market among the participating Member States—clearly enhances a tendency in the need of cross-border data exchanges.

It is not within the scope of this work to investigate or discuss whether the scale of mobility of individuals within the Community is still too small or, rather, it is increasing to significant numbers stimulating the demand side of the business. Instead, the claim is that the task of EU law is to create a level playing field and the conditions for the fulfilment of its goals.

Under this perspective, it becomes apparent that the free movement of people or establishment are affected if individuals cannot access financial facilities for lack of information regarding them in the host Member States in the same way as the nationals or residents of that host Member State. Again, non-discrimination applied to free movement of people and establishment is at stake. In principle, EU nationals or residents should not face barriers caused by the lack of information provided by credit bureaus or different selection criteria used in the hosting Member State.

Similarly, short-term consumption on credit in another Member State is not satisfied either. This would not imply the taking up of legal residence in another Member State but it will be sufficient when consumers travel temporarily and buy goods or receive services in another Member State.[24]

4.4.2 EU Citizenship

To appreciate the matter in full few words on the free movement of people may be helpful.

The free movement right within the EU is one of the four fundamental freedoms forming the foundations of the single market. At first, this freedom was limited to workers and entailed the right to move to another Member State and to live there as a prerequisite to access the job market. A number of social and ancillary rights were the natural corollary to remove the barriers and disadvantages to the worker

---

[24] *Watson v Belmann* (Case C-118/75) [1976] ECR 1185, [1976] 2 CMLR 552; *Luisi v Ministero del Tesoro* (Case C-286/82), [1984] ECR 377, [1985] 3 CMLR 52; *Commission v Netherlands* (Case C-68/89) [1991] ECR I-2637, [1993] 2 CMLR 389. Note that the impact of citizenship rights is also felt in this area of EU Law. See e.g. *Carpenter* (Case C-60/00) [2002] ECR I-6279 C-71/02.

arising from the exercise of the right of free movement in order to ensure that the migrant and his/her family members integrate into the host Member State.[25]

The freedoms of movement and residence granted under Article 45 TFEU (ex Article 39 TEC), together with the related social and other ancillary rights, were also granted to the self-employed and entrepreneurs in the exercise of the right of establishment and to provide services within the EU, and any restrictions on such freedoms have been abolished accordingly.[26]

Until recently, the free movement rights focused on the movement of those economically active. Finally, however, the EU has moved away from this position and expanded the right of free movement in an internal market that allows the free movement of all persons. Thus, not only the economically active ones but all nationals and the lawfully migrant residents of the Member States now benefit from such a right. In particular, Article 21 TFEU (ex 18 TEC) provides that every citizen of the Community shall have the right to move and reside freely within the territory of the Member States.

Secondary legislation gives effect to said free movement and residence of persons: Directive 2004/38/EC, also known as the Citizenship Directive, drawing on early Community legislation as well as the relevant jurisprudence and wide interpretations of the CJEU, has renewed and integrated the earlier framework. Importantly, as said, it applies to all European citizens and legitimate third-country nationals irrespective of any test of economic sufficiency, removing restrictions on the movement and residence of natural persons within the Union.[27] Consequently, the rights contained in the citizenship provisions extend the network of protection

---

[25] Article 45 TFEU (ex Article 39 TEC).

As required under Article 45(3)(d) TFEU (ex Article 39(3)(d) TEC) and Article 46 TFEU (ex Article 40 TEC), secondary legislation was introduced to give substance to the free movement of workers. Principal interventions include Directive 68/360/EEC, OJ L 257 p 0013-0016, governing rights of entry and residence; Regulation 1612/68, OJ L 257 p 0002-0012, governing access to, and conditions of, employment; Regulation 1251/70 OJ L 142 p 0024-0026, governing rights to remain in the territory of a Member State after having been employed there; Directive 64/221/EEC OJ L 56 p 0850-0857, governing Member States' right to derogate from the free movement provisions on the grounds of public policy, public security, or public health. Such measures were later repealed or updated by the so-called Citizenship Directive 2004/38/EC, *infra* below at note n. 26. The term 'worker' has been broadly construed by the following jurisprudence of the Court of Justice of the EU (ex European Court of Justice). See *Hoekstra v BBDA* (Case C-75/63) [1964] ECR 177, [1964] CMLR 319; *Levin v Staatssecretaris van Justitie* (Case C-53/81) [1982] ECR 1035, [1982] 2 CMLR 454; *Kempf v Staatssecretaris van Justitie* (Case C-139/85) [1986] EC 1741, [1987] 1 CMLR 764. For the free movement of students see *Brown v Secretary of State for Scotland* (Case C-197/86) [1988] ECR 3205, [1988] 3 CMLR 403; *Lair v Universitat Hannover* (Case C-39/86) [1989] ECR 3161, [1989] 3 CMLR 545. See also Directive 93/96/EC OJ L 317 p. 0059-0060 now replaced by the Citizenship Directive 2004/38/EC, *infra* below at note n. 26.

[26] Articles 49-54 TFEU (ex Articles 43-48 TEC) provide for the right of establishment. Articles 56-62 TFEU (ex Articles 49-55 TEC) establish the right to provide services.

[27] Directive 2004/38/EC, OJ L 317 p 0059-0060. Grounds for derogation are public security, public health, and public policy.

offered to all European citizens who now enjoy the same related social and ancillary rights as the nationals of the host Member State.[28]

From its inception the EC Treaty expressly made discrimination on the grounds of nationality illegal.[29] A common requisite in the free movement provisions and the achievement of the single market, including in retail finance, is the prohibition of all form of discrimination on the grounds of nationality, both direct and indirect. Such a prohibition has been central to the interpretation and development of the law throughout the years.

From the start, the CJEU has adopted a very broad approach to the issue, including the challenge to rules which were not unequivocally discriminatory but which still had an adverse impact on people's ability to exercise their free movement rights. The prohibition of discrimination, in fact, applies to any rules which, although expressed to operate without distinction, constitute a barrier to the free movement rights.[30] It has a twofold purpose: it concerns both professional and personal rights. Together with the former rights, in fact, the law covers all social advantages whether or not attached to contracts of employment.[31]

In the case of a provider of a service under Articles 56 and 57 TFEU, the matter is less clear as far as it concerns the right to claim full equality other than access to, and conditions of, work in the host Member State. The related freedom to receive services, however, imposes an equal treatment also of personal rights, at least as far as it concerns rights apt to provide/receive in the host Member State those services on a temporary basis free from discrimination on the grounds of nationality.[32]

---

[28] *Baumbast v R* (Case C-413/99) [2002] ECR I-7091; *Martinez Sala v Freistaat Bayern* (Case C-85/96) [1998] ECR I-2691; *Collins v Secretary of State of Work and Pensions* (Case C-138/02) [2005] QB 145, [2004] 3 WLR 1236, [2004] ALL ER (EC) 1005; *Trojani v Le Centre Public d'Aide Sociale de Bruxelles* (Case C-456/02) [2003] C-144/13.

[29] Article 18 TFEU (ex Article 12 TEC).

[30] *Union Royale Belge des Sociétés de Football Association v Bosman* (Case C-415/93) [1995] ECR I-4921, [1996] 1 CMLR 645.

[31] *Ministère Public v Even* (Case C-207/78) [1979] ECR 2019, [1980] 2 CMLR 71.

Of particular interest for the subject matter of this work is *Reina v Landeskreditbank Baden-Wurttemberg* (Case C-65/81) [1982] ECR 33, [1982] 1 CMLR 744. An Italian couple living in Germany claimed a special State-financed childbirth loan from a bank, which was however payable only to German nationals living in Germany. The bank claimed that the loan was not a social benefit as it was not granted as a social right and in any event was granted as every other loan on a discretionary basis (arguing that the difference in treatment was justified on account of the practical difficulties of recovering loans from workers later returning to their home country). The CJEU (ex ECJ) held that the loan should have been granted by reason of the claimant's objective status and that social advantages covered not only benefits granted as of right but also those granted on a discretionary basis.

Similarly, see *Commission v Italy* (Case C-63/86) [1986] ECR 29, [1988] CMLR 16 where it was held that a discounted mortgage facility available to Italian nationals was in breach of then Art. 7 EEC, now Article 18 TFEU (ex Article 12 TEC), and therefore should have been made available on a basis of equality to all residing EC nationals in Italy.

[32] *Gravier v City of Liège* (Case C-293/83) [1985] ECR 593, [1985] 3 CMLR 1; *Luisi v Ministero del Tesoro* (Case C-286/82), cit. *supra* at note n. 23.

The Citizenship Directive now clarifies any doubt. It extends the provisions of equality of treatment and related jurisprudential interpretations to all Community citizens and third-country nationals lawfully residing, as well as providing or receiving services, in the territory of the host Member State.[33]

In conclusion, thus, the impact of the concept of citizenship can be observed in full on the prohibition of discrimination based on nationality, enabling those who move and reside within the EU to enjoy the same treatment in law irrespective of their nationality, where direct or indirect barriers to such free movement provisions shall be removed.[34]

Another side of the same coin is the situation where a national of a Member State moves to another Member State and, after some time, moves back to his or her home Member State. He or she will find himself or herself in the same position of a migrant from another Member State.

4.4.3   Non-Discrimination in Access to Services

At this point of the discussion, a clarification becomes necessary. No law or regulation provides for the right to credit, either in terms of straight professional or personal right.

Arguably, nevertheless, access to finance constitutes a precondition for the equality of treatment among EU citizens and lawful third-country nationals to fully enjoy the rights granted by the Community freedoms. At the very least, when a national or resident of a Member State applies for finance to a lender in another Member State, whether in the exercise of the freedom of movement right or the right to receive services, he/she should benefit from exactly the same treatment that nationals of the host Member State enjoy. For example, a consumer lawfully resident in another Member State should be able to buy goods or receive services at the same terms and conditions as anyone else, including the possibility of taking advantage of the credit/instalment purchase facilities on offer. It would be discriminatory in practice to offer better deals to people only on the basis of nationality or previous residency, especially if one considers that a number of expensive goods on many occasions may be purchased only on credit terms.

This may increasingly imping in the online environment and the growth of e-commerce in a digital single market.

---

[33] Directive 2004/38/EC, cit. *supra* at note n. 26. Such extension has some limitations applying to those who are not economically active (excluding family members of economically active ones) as far as it concerns social assistance during the first three months of residence or while seeking work.

[34] Some of the most interesting cases on the repercussions of citizenship can be observed in *Grzelczyk* (Case C-184/99) [2001] ECR I-6193; *Collins v Secretary of State of Work and Pensions* (Case C-138/02), cit. *supra* at note n. 27; *Ioannidis* (Case C-258/04) [2005] 3 CMLR 47.

Any direct or indirect barrier to achieve equality of treatment or opportunity, therefore, should be removed. The information infrastructure may become an indirect form of discrimination that undermines the full enjoyment of the basic Union freedoms and their corollaries.

4.5 Regulatory Failures and the Role of Competition in the Information Market

4.5.1 General

The previous sections have emphasised that there appears to be an inconsistency in the promotion of the internal market and competition among lenders on the one side, and an information infrastructure and market that remain national on the other side.

The legislative efforts of the CCD and the MCD to integrate markets risk remaining an empty letter and, as they stand, they are unlikely to enhance cross-border credit, either as cross-border provision of services, consumer consumption abroad, or EU migration and access to important services in host Member States.

The EU relevance and dimension of the exchange of information, coupled with the other policy objectives that it aims to achieve, seem to suggest that the state of affairs cannot remain a national business for longer. However, there seem to be little prospects of the information market of growing European for being structured to work at national level, at least within the framework of the existing lack of interoperability among national systems and the institutional arrangements serving the underlying financial market.

Regulatory failures appear evident, but the decision of the CJEU in *Asnef* and the *2011 Guidelines* not only are of little help in this prospect, but they may make the situation worse.

By legitimising national exchanges of default information, but failing to investigate further away the full EU dimension of credit for consumers, information markets, and the effects on trade between Member States, *Asnef* and the *2011 Guidelines* risk leaving in place—or even consecrating—a vacuum with repercussions on competition and EU market integration. With all the practical difficulties of the case, competition risks to be seen as a matter limited to establishing a commercial presence in a Member State where the same safeguards are not provided for cross-border modes on either the demand or supply side. If lenders need to have a physical presence in a Member State to become a member of the information exchange system and comply with reciprocity principles, this could arguably represent a barrier and account as an anticompetitive practice.

If, by contrast, it is opposed that participation in systems that, in the decided case-law, are voluntary is not critical for risk management and competition, then this recognition would undermine the very same theory upon which the whole information system relies on and finds its justifications, hence its existence. Either information exchanges do really address risk management and are pro-competitive or the whole system is flawed at its roots and would not justify those assumptions or foundations upon which the judgement and existing guidelines are premised.

Whatever the argument, recent studies point out that to the extent that credit reporting is capable of affecting the modes of entry of financial institutions, it may well influence the strategic behaviour of existing market players and the use of private credit bureaus could be more prone to strategic behaviour rather than risk management.[35]

Therefore, without a proper European exchange system with uniform or compatible information, or interoperable systems, an integrated and competitive market at EU level remains an impracticable goal.[36] Likewise, the lack of interoperability or compatibility of the legal form or institutional structure of credit bureaus in the Member States risk undermining both the information market and the underlying consumer financial sector.

Hypothetically, for the wider policy objectives that are at stake in a number of Member States, this would be possible through public institutions that may exchange information between them, a circumstance technically possible and happening for the exchange of information on loans to enterprises.[37] From this angle, *Asnef* and the *2011 Guidelines* appear probably misguiding and most certainly a missed opportunity in this direction.

4.5.2 Any Role for Competition Policy and Law?

Without a doubt, regulatory failures at EU level outside strict competition law bear the responsibility of such a state of affairs. Probably, sector-specific legislation would best address the many problems. But the EU legislator has already failed to address the two intertwined markets, as demonstrated by the latest experience of the MCD.

At the same time, on their side the judiciary and the European Commission have had an opportunity to dig into the problems of the market at study. But they have taken a too narrow approach towards competition law, looking exclusively at competition in one market but not in the other, moreover failing to make necessary distinctions that do have an impact on the serving market.

---

[35] A voluntary system also provides an incentive to strategically report incomplete information on their good clients to deter others to attract them. See Giannetti et al. (2010), Bouckaert and Degryse (2004), pp. 27–52; Bouckaert and Degryse (2006), pp. 702–720; Gehrig and Stenbacka (2007), pp. 77–99.

[36] It should be acknowledged that the Commission mandated an Expert Group on Credit Histories to look at ways to facilitate the cross-border exchange of credit data. The report failed to find consensus and consumer organisation refused to underwrite it. See European Commission (2009). Nothing came out from the Report in policy or legislative terms. The Report remains a controversial document both in content and in its recommendations.

[37] Deutsche Bundesbank (2005).

Yet, competition policy and law may play a key role if the discussion does not remain limited to competition among lenders in the exchange of information but it is also transferred or extended to competition in the underlying information market and industry.

This work has already repeated many times that, although not always appreciated by some economic literature, the integration of national markets features prominently in EU competition policy and law. In addition, the CJEU has already established that it is the task of competition law to protect the structure of the market and, in so doing, competition as such.[38]

Behaviours that undermine the efforts to achieve an integrated EU internal market are liable to infringe the norms of competition law.

Competition law enforcement in the information industry may provide a useful contribution.

4.6 Competition in the Information Industry

4.6.1 Hub-and-Spoke Agreements

One of the possible reasons why the information industry has not specifically come under the close scrutiny of competition law enforcement may be related with its role of third party provider in the reference market of loans for consumers.

As seen in the previous Chapter, traditionally an exchange of information among competitors is looked vis-à-vis the competitive or anti-competitive object or effect on those making use of the information in the market for consumer loans, not on those providing information.

However, the reference market may be affected in many ways. Clearly, there is the element of the competition among lenders; yet, this involves not only the covered horizontal relations between the lenders themselves, but also the vertical relation between the lenders and the credit bureaus. Moreover, when commercial entities are involved, horizontal relations between information providers may become relevant.

But in situations where two markets are intertwined and one market serves the other, why not looking at both markets and any resulting vertical relationship?

The answer may find its roots in the traditional treatment of the so-called 'hub and spoke' agreements, which already fall within the scope of the existing competition rules of Article 101 TFEU discussed previously in Chap. 3.

Hub and spoke agreements have been playfully referred to as "the vertical expression of a horizontal desire" in the same fashion as a sensual tango dance, with all insinuations to other endeavours this illustration may authorise.[39] As

---

[38] *GlaxoSmithKline Services Unlimited v Commission* (Joined cases C-501/06 P, C-513/06 P, C-515/06 P, and C-519/06 P) [2009] ECR I-9291, para 63.

[39] See Chillin' Competition Blog, "The vertical expression of a horizontal desire" at http://chillingcompetition.com/2012/03/28/the-vertical-expression-of-a-horizontal-desire/.

colourful as this expression may be, it gives well the idea that these are ordinary vertical agreements but with potential horizontal anti-competitive effects. Precisely as in the case at study, they involve an exchange of information between two or more undertakings operating at the same level of the production or distribution chain via a common contractual partner operating at a different level of the chain.

The European Commission, in its *Guidelines on Vertical Restraints*, had already expressed the concern that such indirect flows of information could be used as a substitute to replicate information exchanges that would be prohibited if they occurred directly.[40]

At the same time, when looking at horizontal agreements the same European Commission notes that, while its *2011 Guidelines* do not specifically address hub and spoke infringements, the general principles therein set out apply equally to this type of arrangements, acknowledging that infringing information exchanges may occur indirectly through a common agency such as a trade association or other third parties or through the companies' suppliers or retailers.

However, any possible liability of the vertical participant in an information exchange has not yet been examined under EU Competition law, and national cases in the Member States confirm the trend.[41]

4.6.2 Side Effects of Vertical Integration

To the extent that information is turned into a tradable commodity of commercial value, nonetheless any possible competition issues or interferences of such intertwined markets have not yet been addressed.

This work argues that the horizontal competition between the information providers themselves cannot be neglected. The distinction is important because information providers become active market players, especially when private commercial actors are the suppliers, influencing and impacting on the underlying consumer markets in terms of lenders' entry and behaviour, transparency, pricing of loans, and consumers access to financial services.

---

[40] European Commission, Guidelines on Vertical Restraints [2010] OJ C130/1; in particular see para 211 where the European Commission is of the view that "agreements may facilitate collusion between distributors when the same supplier serves as a category captain for all or most of the competing distributors on a market and provides these distributors with a common point of reference for their marketing decisions".

[41] *Coöperatieve Vereniging 'Suiker Unie' Ua v Commission* (Joined Cases 40–48, 50, 54–56, 111, 113, 114–73) [1975] ECR 1663. In the UK, see for example Office of Fair Trading (OFT) Decision of 1 August 2003 into Price-fixing of *Replica Football Kits* [2003] Case CP/0871/01; OFT Decision of 21 November 2003 into Agreements between *Hasbro UK Ltd, Argos Ltd, and Littlewoods Ltd* [2003] Case CP/0480–01; *Allsports Limited v Office of Fair Trading* [2004] CAT 17; *JJB Sports plc v Office of Fair Trading* [2006] EWCA Civ 1318; *Dairy Tesco v Office of Fair Trading* [2012] CAT 31.

It is true that Article 101 TFEU prohibits not only restrictive agreements at the same level of the economy, i.e. horizontal agreements, but also at different levels of the distribution chain, i.e. vertically, and relating to the conditions under which the parties may sell their goods or services.[42] However, the vertical relationship between lenders and credit bureaus, alongside the implication of competition among the credit bureaus themselves, has been left unexplored by the judiciary when it had such an opportunity in *Asnef*. Equally, the *2011 Guidelines* are not helpful either. If anything, they leave in place another conundrum of difficult resolution which, arguably, does not contribute to that clarity and legal certainty that would be required.

In conclusion, what derives under current European competition law enforcement is that the role of credit bureaus in possible competitive or anti-competitive behaviours remains absorbed by that of the financial institutions as horizontal participants, where the liability of the bureau as vertical participant is not considered, or the horizontal competition among these information providers evaluated.

Yet, hub-and-spoke may well pose enforcement problems specific to these kind of arrangements that go further than the traditional approach.

For example, recently US competition law has started to address the liability and enforcement on the vertical participant in an information exchange.[43]

Only recently, new literature has started questioning whether this jurisprudence is appropriately applied in the vertical sphere advancing the proposition that further investigation and analysis would be required to address all the complex matters arising out of hub-and-spoke relationships.[44]

At least, what it appears is that hub-and-spoke pose some new challenges and additional enforcement problems that require further reflection.

Actually, some economic literature has already shown awareness of anti-competitive problems relating to such a vertical or hub-and-spoke relationship in consumer financial markets beyond the traditional analysis: it has been demonstrated how credit bureaus may well be used by dominant lenders as concerted practices to raise rivals' costs either downstream for new market players, or upstream for possible rival credit bureaus that cannot obtain data from lenders.[45]

This is what happens in several EU Member States where only one credit bureau at national level pools consumer financial data,[46] which risks having the undesirable effect of financial institutions becoming vertically integrated with one

---

[42] On vertical agreements see Commission Regulation (EU) No. 330/2010 of 20 April 2010 on the application of Article 101(3) TFEU to categories of vertical agreements and concerted practices, OJ No. L 102 of 23 April 2010, p. 1. See also cases *Consten and Grundig vs Commission* (Joined Cases 56/64 and 58/64 of 13 July 1966) [1966] ECR 299.

[43] See, for example, *US v Apple* et al. 12 Civ. 2826 (July 10, 2013).

[44] Odudu (2011), pp. 205–242.

[45] Giannetti et al. (2010).

[46] European Commission, "Report on the retail banking sector inquiry", *Commission Staff Working Document accompanying the Communication from the Commission—Sector Inquiry under Art 17 of Regulation 1/2003 on retail banking (Final Report)* [COM(2007) 33 final] SEC(2007) 106; European Commission (2009).

credit bureau, often of commercial nature. As noted earlier, this is so because participation, coverage and accuracy are intertwined in the same essence of an information system, which would not make any sense if incomplete, i.e. when participation and coverage are not universal, in turn translating into inaccuracy. However, as a dog biting its own tail, in turn accuracy is a key feature of a legitimate pro-competitive information exchange. Hence, the pieces of the puzzle do not easily come in their place.

The vertical integration in the information industry introduces the issue of foreclosures and dominance in the information market, that in most Member States is a business affair of private or commercial entities doing business as any other companies.

4.7 Networks and Information Monopolies

4.7.1 Networks

Each market has different characteristics which influence the behaviour and strategies of its participants. Information markets are relatively new, at least in terms of its commodification and commercialisation. Where in the past information materialised in the product that was commercialised (e.g. books, DVDs, etc.), with the expansion of information technologies and the digital economy it has acquired its own value regardless of the medium where it is incorporated. Financial information and its exchange is a classic example of a commodity turned into a tradable service with its own market.

As noted in the Chap. 3 and briefly recalled in the final part of the above Section, in the market at study the relationship between accuracy, verification/vetting of information, coverage, and participation or outreach is central for the proper functioning of the information system itself, as well as for competition and its rules. A partial data sharing would underpin the whole foundations upon which the system itself is grounded. Also, it would undermine the assumptions upon which the CJEU rely in its decisions, as well as those of the European Commission in its *2011 Guidelines*.

Accuracy is the key for a lawful information exchange under competition law but, to be accurate and to function properly, an information system should have a very broad coverage, ideally universal.

Credit bureaus operate through a network structure. This takes the form of a simple star network with a central hub, where such a hub must be sized appropriately to accommodate demand in the market.[47] It occurs at horizontal level with lenders providing the data, which in turn are pooled vertically in the database organised and owned by the credit bureaus themselves.

---

[47] Fatur (2011).

Indeed, competition in the information exchange industry is closely tied with the economics of networks, according to which the value of services depends on the number of subscribers.[48]

A common trait that these systems share is that, in economic terms, they are natural monopolies in that the extension of a system's coverage itself enhances its effectiveness. In fact, they are dependent on that network structures within which information is traded, where the participants that share the information constitute such a network.[49]

The achievement of economies of scale is essential for coverage, where scale and scope effects affect coverage which has the propensity to universality, thus concentration. Historically, for example, the need to achieve economies of scale with nationwide market coverage was the main reason behind the concentration process that occurred in the US after an initial period of numerous credit bureaus spread over the nation's territory to serve local business communities.[50]

Economic research describes such networks as a form of industrial organisation and market governance, where they can influence market structure, and the behaviour of firms and their performance, hence competition. Accordingly, in credit reporting markets, the information flows among agencies, information suppliers and consumers constitute a network of information whose value increases as more lenders are connected to it. Consequently, the more the network of one credit bureau increases, the more attractive it becomes for potential participants or participants to other networks. Therefore, to the extent that scale and scope effects also affect coverage, the more sources are connected to the network, the more detailed becomes the credit report and knowledge, and the more precise may become for risk-management purposes.[51]

This ultimately raises the question of freedom to contract or negotiate with dominant information providers by the participants themselves. The question is whether any market player may be left out from the system if and to the extent that the benefits are such as those claimed by the industry and taken as economic assumptions by the judiciary and policy makers alike.

Likewise, the question arises whether small players in retail financial markets may afford to remain out of the network; again, a positive answer would undermine the economic assumptions upon which the exchange of information is premised. A negative answer, by contrast, would exemplify how the behaviour of firms can be biased by a vertically integrated dominant company.

In short, the very nature of the consumer financial information business demands that the success of the system depends on its universal extension, otherwise it would be of little or no use, and the whole legal architecture upon which legitimacy is claimed would collapse. But the issue of universal coverage in

---

[48] Rohlfs (1974), pp. 16–37; Fatur (2011), Jentzsch (2006).

[49] Pagano and Jappelli (1993), pp. 1693-1718.

[50] Ibid. See also Olegario (2003), pp. 115–159.

[51] Jentzsch (2003, 2006).

a commercial context poses inter alia questions relating to free competition both for the participants and the information suppliers themselves.

The circumstances are different where the information hub is a public institution pursuing identified policy objectives and operating as a regulator rather than a voluntary commercial venture. Here, the hub acts as regulator or authority under the rule of law, but this does not necessarily impede that the information exchange serves inter alia competitive purpose.

4.8 Monopolies and Article 102 TFEU

4.8.1 In General: Abuse of Dominant Position

Monopolies or oligopolies are not anti-competitive by definition. On the contrary, they may be perfectly legitimate from an economic and legal point of view.

Nevertheless, few aspects require attention when private commercial companies become involved as information providers like in the case of credit bureaus that inter alia have been the object of an important CJEU decision in the sector and informed the latest guidelines on the matter.

It has already been pointed out the potential problems of their vertical integration with the lenders. At the same time, the monopolistic or oligopolistic nature of commercial organisations at national level raises the issues of lack of horizontal competition among them, the partitioning of the EU market into national markets, the absence of interoperability among their information systems, and the maintenance of obstacles to EU market integration.

At first sight, such architecture or market behaviour may have the potential to be caught by Article 102 TFEU, which prohibits any abuse by one or more undertakings of a dominant position within the internal market in so far as it may affect trade between Member States.[52]

The essence of this provision is to control market power once one or more undertakings have acquired a dominant position in relation to a particular market,

---

[52] According to Article 102 TFEU, "Any abuse by one or more undertakings of a dominant position within the internal market or in a substantial part of it shall be prohibited as incompatible with the internal market in so far as it may affect trade between Member States.

Such abuse may, in particular, consist in:

(a) directly or indirectly imposing unfair purchase or selling prices or other unfair trading conditions;

(b) limiting production, markets or technical development to the prejudice of consumers;

(c) applying dissimilar conditions to equivalent transactions with other trading parties, thereby placing them at a competitive disadvantage;

(d) making the conclusion of contracts subject to acceptance by the other parties of supplementary obligations which, by their nature or according to commercial usage, have no connection with the subject of such contracts.

i.e. a clearly identified geographical area where a product or service is marketed and the conditions of competitions are sufficiently homogeneous.[53]

However, Article 102 TFEU does not prohibit dominance per se, but the abuse of such a dominant position is required, albeit no causal link between the two is required.[54]

Thus, it is commonly represented that for a violation of Article 102 TFEU to occur, the four cumulative four conditions need to be met:

(1) A dominant position on the relevant market by one or more undertakings;
(2) Such a position must be held in the internal market or substantial part of it;
(3) There has to be an abuse of such a dominant position;
(4) There are actual or potential effects on trade between Member States.[55]

On the matters of dominance and the reference market of credit bureaus, much has been already written so far. Likewise, on the effects on inter-state trade and integration it has been pointed out at length how the market organisation and the conduct of information suppliers impact on the structure of competition. Moreover, this is a concept that is applied broadly and any potential cross-border effect is usually sufficient for EU competition law enforcement.[56]

The requisite of 'abuse' may be a more challenging one to assess. There are several aspects to the concept of abuse, each one discussed at length in the literature.[57] All that can be said here is that to be abusive, a dominant undertaking needs to engage in an activity that negatively affects market structure and consumer welfare. This is a difficult analysis to undertake that requires the assessment of many variables and the specificities of each reference market.

This work does not have the ambition to make a case-by-case assessment of possible Article 102 TFEU infringements by national credit bureaus, which remain a detailed analysis to be carried out with all the elements and complexities of the relevant markets. Nor it puts forward that commercial credit bureaus automatically fall short of competition law enforcement under Article 102 TFEU.

More modestly, the suggestion is that the competition in the sector may be far more problematic than that presented so far by the EU judiciary and by the European Commission, and that a broader approach may be necessary.

To the extent that abusive exclusionary conducts are used by dominant undertakings to protect or extend their dominant position, it becomes important to assess both exclusion from the same market and exclusion from a vertically integrated market, where the hardest issue is to distinguish between anti-competitive and pro-competitive foreclosure. The competition authorities will intervene under Article

---

[53] Lista (2013), O'Donoghue and Padilla (2013).

[54] *Europemballage Corporation and Continental Can Company v Commission* (Case 6/72) [1973] ECR 215.

[55] Whish (2012), Lorenz (2013), Graham (2010).

[56] Ibid.

[57] For e.g. a detailed and comprehensive account is provided by O'Donoghue and Padilla (2013).

102 TFEU if there are coherent explanations of how the allegedly abusive conduct results in consumer harm or the fragmentation of the EU single market.

This work has shown above how credit bureaus bear a responsibility for the fragmentation of both EU markets in consumer finance and in financial information.

Whether and to what extent they make the interest of consumers is a determination that may be more complex than the one superficially undertaken by the authorities in the context of Art. 101 TFEU already discussed in Chap. 3.

The consumer interest or harm in the context of financial information and its exchange will be covered in more detail in Chap. 5.

4.8.2 Markets Where Competition May not be Feasible

It is worth a reflection that there are markets where conventional competition is not feasible, such as markets that are natural monopolies precisely in the sense that economies of scale and scope are so large that only one firm may supply the market at reasonable cost efficiency.[58]

In these circumstances, it is usually necessary to intervene with specific sector regulation, e.g. prices, investments, service quality, etc., or through the regulatory intervention of a vertical separation.[59] For example, as in the case of the electricity market where there may be a separation of ownership of electricity generation and the distribution network, similarly the same could be applied to the ownership of databases and the distribution of information.

Better still, the European industry knows already the model of public credit bureaus, studied earlier in Chap. 2. That could well be an existing example of a regulator taking charge of such a natural monopoly, where inter alia such public institutions have the knowledge and technological abilities to engage in cross-border exchanges of information. Public credit bureaus in Europe had already finalised a plan for a pan-European data exchange among their databases of Belgium, Germany, France, Italy, Austria, Portugal, and Spain, as well as representatives of the European Central Bank. The plan consists in the creation of:

> a reporting system that allows data exchange on a regular basis. The credit register of country A will then receive information from the register in other countries on borrowers who also have debt in other European countries. (...) National financial institutions, on the other hand, are supposed to gain access to borrower information of other countries via their own credit registry.[60]

---

[58] Lyons (2009), pp. 1–26. The author makes the example of the major distributional infrastructures like electricity, gas, or water networks (sp. 11) but the concept may be applied to the case at study. See also Graham (2010), sp. Chap. 12.

[59] Ibid.

[60] Jentzsch and San José Riestra (2003), sp. 22–23. Also in Jentzsch (2006), sp. 45.

Sure, the envisaged cross-border exchange was not intended for the consumer sector but to provide information to financial institutions across Europe about the indebtedness of their corporate customers.[61]

At the same time, what it shows is that the relevant authorities have already developed a communication network among them, where appropriate cooperation is already in place without the hurdle to create a system from nowhere.[62] The major problem behind the creation of interfaces among the information systems would remain that of system interoperability, which should be left to EU regulatory intervention.

4.8.3 System Interoperability and Lock-Ins

Because of the rapid growth of the digital sector and the swift acquisition of market power and the natural dominance of networks, competition authorities have started to scrutinise more closely some market practices of this type of industrial organisation. So far, this has mostly occurred in the computer, software and internet domains, where the value of a product largely depends on the extent to which it can be used together with systems that consumers already have.[63]

Some corresponding substantial literature has started to emerge.[64]

In the information society the main concern of the European competition authorities has been to tackle anti-competitive practices due to the inability of technology products to communicate in networks with other IT products (again, known as 'interoperability'). Such practices have the potential of interlocking customers and foreclosing competitors, reducing consumer choice and ultimately affecting innovation. This is a complex area of study that involves discussions over proprietary rights of companies, licensing of technologies not protected by

---

[61] As explicitly documented by the Deutsche Bundesbank (the Central Bank chairing the Working Group on Credit Registries), in fact, "data on the total amount of loans taken up will be available for each of the participating countries as well as on an aggregated basis. The data will also provide a breakdown into asset items and off balance-sheet transactions. *There will be no cross-border exchange of information on loans to individuals*" (emphasis added). See Deutsche Bundesbank (2005).

[62] Additionally, the existing technologies in use in the sector support the view that, for such a system to be complemented, radical organisational or innovative measures would not be required. Certainly, there may be one-off costs in the adaptation of existing systems or the creation of new ones for countries that may have a different system in place.

[63] Graef (2014), pp. 6–19.

[64] Coates (2011), Fatur (2011).

obligatory standards, regulatory choices and policy options under the future digital agenda of the EU, and the like.[65]

However, whilst software interoperability has been on the spotlight, a market with similar features such as the one at study has remained in the shadow despite the opportunity that was presented to the authorities in *Asnef* and in the drafting of the *2011 Guidelines*.

Probably, placing such a demand on the judiciary would have been over-ambitious. But, narrowing down to the exchange of financial information, and bearing in mind the specific features of the sector, there are nonetheless traits of communal interest that may be transferred in discussions over competition.

Credit bureaus provide information systems and technologies that include any equipment or interconnected system in the acquisition, processing, storage, manipulation, control, display, transmission and reception, etc. of data. This requirement occurs for both the demand and the supply side of the market. Information systems are usually highly sophisticated. The initial high costs to develop technologies and set up a network, coupled with the issue of market coverage, create strong concentration in the information industry. Companies are unlikely to share specifications implemented in a system that enables intercon-nections with other services, especially in the absence of obligatory standards set by regulation. As in a vicious circle, standard settings outside a regulatory umbrella may in turn pose problems for competition authorities because legally a standard constitutes an agreement between companies.[66]

Another related feature is the interdependency or lock-in of customers. As soon as financial institutions join a system they have to conform to its reporting stan-dards, software, type, breath and detail of information, protocols, etc. Also, staff needs to be trained to use the system and procedures need to be set up. All of this would make it costly and unnecessary to switch to a competing provider and its system. Entry foreclosures of competing systems become likely.

With all due differences regarding the market, technologies in place, and the range of customers, the above narrative suggests that there may be some resem-blance with recent high-profile antitrust cases in the high-tech sector.

In the *Microsoft* case, much of the discussion centered on the factual question of whether or not interoperability between operating systems was limited. It was

---

[65] The European Commission has studied the possible introduction of new legal measures to improve software interoperability but it concluded that legal intervention was not appropriate. See European Commission, Communication from the Commission to the European Parliament, the Council, the European Economic and Social Committee and the Committee of the Regions— A Digital Agenda for Europe, COM (2010) 245 final, available at http://eur-lex.europa.eu/ legal-content/EN/ALL/;jsessionid=dmKpTG3hGG13pMsFy2LVZCvnG2Nzb1Lb4g2ZDJnCDPp wnJYzvx7M!1011527203?uri=CELEX:52010DC0245R(01); European Commission, Commis-sion Staff Working Document—Analysis of measures that could lead significant market players in the ICT sector to license interoperability information, SWD (2013) 209 final, available from http://ec.europa.eu/digital-agenda/en/news/analysis-measures-could-lead-significant-market-players-ict-sector-license-interoperability. See also Graef (2014), pp. 6–19.

[66] Schellingerhout (2011), pp. 3–9.

found that interlocking monopoly systems and products based on its proprietary Windows system allowed the company to prevent the interoperability of competing products. Microsoft was ordered to provide essential interoperability information to allow the development of competing products.[67]

Therefore, access obligations may include granting open access to technical interfaces, protocols or other important technologies that are indispensable for the interoperability of network services.

Interoperability restrictions by a dominant company may be justified only by efficiency benefits that are gained from restricting the access to the system.

From the Microsoft case, the position of the European Commission is clear in that for an abuse to exist it must have a foreclosing effect in the tied market, the tying market, or both. The importance of economies of scale and network effects can result in costs and other impediments faced by customers if or when switching to a new provider because the latter may not have a large base of customers. In conclusion, in similar situations there is awareness of the risk of anti-competitive foreclosure where technical tying is in place, which is a circumstance credit bureaus are not exempted.[68]

As reminded by the emerging literature, interoperability is not a goal in itself but a means to achieve other goals such as competition, consumer choice and innovation.[69]

A refusal or practical impediment to provide competitors with access to interoperable information may thus fall within the scope of abuse of dominance under Article 102 TFEU.

4.9 Personal Information and Competition

4.9.1 Secondary Uses of Information and Additional Services

Very few people would dissent with the fashionable yet authoritative vision of information as "the oil of the new economy".[70]

Even if this metaphor was used with reference to the importance of the digital economy and information technologies for economic growth, it is self-evident how precious information is especially for marketing intended in its broadest sense, from decision making on strategies to pricing.

As noticed in Chap. 2, commercial credit bureaus—i.e. organisation working for profit—have exploited the knowledge they organise to the market and they

---

[67] *Microsoft v Commission* (Case T-201) [2004] ECR II-4463.

[68] European Commission, Communication from the Commission, Guidance on the Commission's Enforcement Priorities in applying Article 82 of the EC Treaty to abusive exclusionary conduct by dominant undertakings, C (2009) 864 final (Brussels, 9 February 2009).

[69] Graef (2014), pp. 6–19.

[70] Kuneva (2009)

have developed a number of additional products for the same client base that they serve for their traditional business.

For example, they provide their clients with additional services such as statistical models to produce and sell credit scoring services by which they rate borrowers according to their credit history and profile derived from the processing of information from different other data sources. Where a wide range of data is available, as it is in most cases, the models may be intensively and increasingly used for purposes other than the assessment of borrowers' creditworthiness. Examples include scoring customers to promote financial products, price loans, manage credit limits and monitor situations to offer other financial products, etc. These have become ordinary practices of financial institutions, sometimes exceeding in aggressive marketing practices. Recently, for example, some of these activities have come in the spotlight for the setting-up of tailored businesses or products to target borrowers with poor credit records, engaging in what has become known as 'subprime lending'.[71]

Most of all, data are the lifeblood for the marketing of the financial industry. Examples of additional products or services may be abundant, from consulting to geo-marking, or from fraud prevention to identity verification tools (NB—the fact that these latter activities are and should remain the prerogative of the State exceeds this discussion but it is nevertheless worth a mention to provide the right perspective of the type of products or services exemplified).

What matters for the discussion under analysis is that, as it happens in every private sector market economy, where companies are driven by the need to make profits and prevail over competitors, credit bureaus are continuously persuaded to study, develop and commercialise new products or services, thus using data mining techniques on personal financial data and other data sources at their disposal.

Information, after all, is their core business and asset. This is where the provision of such additional services, often provided via subsidiaries or controlled companies, may become relevant for competition law enforcement when it is channelled through an existing dominant or monopolistic position.

The problem may be that other market-intelligence firms aiming at entering such a marketing could be foreclosed. To the extent that a dominant company, bearing monopolistic tendencies, engages directly or indirectly in the supply of products or services that are technically tied to the core one and work via its system, this may come under the scrutiny of Article 102 TFEU in the same fashion as that of operating system and software providers touched upon shortly above. For example, Microsoft was condemned for tying one of its products with its ubiquitous operating system.[72]

---

[71] According to *The Economist*, "When the tide goes out" (March 24th–30th 2007), 36, interest rates on such loans are usually at least 50 % higher than those charged to lenders' best customers. See also *The Economist*, "The trouble with the housing market" (March 24th–30th 2007), sp. 11; *The Economist*, "Cracks in the facade" (March 24th–30th 2007), sp. 87–89.

[72] *Microsoft v Commission* (Case T-201), cit. supra at note n. 66.

This does not mean that competition in the financial information sector is necessarily absent. Certainly, for the reasons above explained, the financial information sector is a peculiar one and in several countries only one monopolistic system is in place.

If anything, nevertheless, this shows the potentials of competition foreclosures.

But the reality of a minority of Member States suggests that competition is somehow possible, although looking at the figures the temptation is to move the terminology away from 'monopoly' to 'oligopoly' which does not guarantee a competitive market. In the EU six Member States have two market players, the UK has three, and Sweden has exceptionally six bureaus.[73]

In the described type of market, with such a homogeneous product and service, the way in which the bureaus may potentially compete would be limited to prices, coverage rates, and data quality.[74]

However, as noted earlier, in this kind of market these three elements are a prerequisite for its validity, economic and legal. Thus, the real ground for competition seems to shift from the core activity of distributing consumer information to the additional services that they offer which are built on the secondary uses of the data. As a result, experimentation and development of new products and/or services—based on data mining, manipulation, and further uses of the data—may play a very important competitive role.

4.9.2 Preliminary Issues on Competition and Data Protection

Whatever the economic reasons for having more than one star network in an homogeneous market, which seems at odds with coverage and accuracy and hence a key requisite for a lawful exchange, both the duplication of databases and the secondary uses or manipulation of information raise the fundamental issues of their necessity and data minimisation under data protection law.

Data protection and the relationship with competition policy and law will be analysed in greater detail later in Chap. 5. At this stage, however, for its relevance it is necessary to anticipate that necessity of data processing, proportionality, and data minimisation are pillars of the legal architecture of data protection. Two or more firms trading personal information with a resulting homogeneous product would most probably clash with these principles—or at least they should in principle. If data are to be processed in a manner consistent and proportionate with

---

[73] European Parliament (2011), Responsible Lending—Barriers to Competition, DG for Internal Policies, Economic and Monetary Affairs, Table 3, p. 81–82—IP/A/ECON/ST/2011-05, Brussels: European Parliament.

[74] See Jappelli and Pagano (2006), pp. 347–371.

the legitimate goals to be achieved, what would justify duplications or overlapping of processing for the same purpose or even further uses?

Clearly, a compliance analysis should be carried out in each jurisdiction, but the following existing decision on this theme is significant.

In the context of the enactment of a specific code of conduct for the processing of consumer financial data, the Italian Data Protection Authority have stated that the complex processing operations involving such personal data.

> entail risks for data subjects' fundamental rights and freedoms, as they may negatively affect private life, legitimate access to the purchase of goods and/or the delivery of services, and ultimately individuals' dignity and repute, social and professional relations, and private enterprise.[75]

Therefore, the Italian Authority concludes that it is necessary to avoid duplication and overlapping of databases as well as the proliferation of multiple-industry databases whether centralised or interconnected, which may give rise to an excess of information that is aimed at the most diverse purposes, concerns a high number of people, and may end up being especially intrusive because of the many opportunities for matching data.[76]

What appears relevant for this discussion is that even in those few cases where horizontal competition in the information market exists, competition may not be so simple, especially if there is not a specific regulatory umbrella or it is not exercised by a public authority pursuing shared policy goals in the public interest under the rule of law.

As it will be seen in Chap. 5 and in the Conclusions, the latter model would not be incompatible with the purposes of competition.

4.10 The Consumer-Information Provider Relationship: An Unchartered Territory

As noted in Chap. 2, one of the justifications on competition grounds of the benefits of having credit bureaus is that they reduce the information monopoly of large lenders. Leaving aside any debate over the possible competitive value of market intelligence carried out by market players, as well as the value of their information assets over years of experience, if it is true that competition benefits from the opening of the market to smaller lenders, at the same time it cannot be overlooked that in reality the information monopoly moves to a new undertaking at a different level.

---

[75] Garante per la Protezione dei Dati Personali (Italian Data Protection Authority), "Balancing of interests: data collection by CRAs without consent" (Rome, 16 November 2004), available at http://www.garanteprivacy.it/web/guest/home/docweb/-/docweb-display/docweb/1671380.
[76] Ibid.

In this type of network structure, the consumer is not the direct customer of the hub, but his or her position often remains concealed. In the case at study, any consumers doing business with any lender in an ideally competitive market, where they can choose among a multitude of offers from different suppliers, they end up doing business with a dominant credit bureau, regardless of whether they want it or not, or even whether they know it or not.

This assertion needs specification. Strictly speaking, the consumer does not do any direct business with credit bureaus. Indirectly, however, consumer information is the currency of the credit bureaus business. Credit bureaus make their business with the information pertaining to the consumer, albeit not in a proprietary sense.[77] By doing business with any lender in the market, consumer data are pooled in a dominant company whose provision of information to all lenders will determine the same consumer future transactions, affecting him or her at later stages in a manner unknown to them at the time of the first transaction. Credit information becomes the gateway to credit, access to other goods and services, and other essentials.

In short, through a variety of providers of retail finance chosen by the consumers, the latter flow into the bottleneck of a third-party company without a choice or the possibility to refuse, unless they do not want to see their application being rejected. This third-party company, in turn, will control the information that will influence all other firms and will ultimately affect for the good or for the bad access the consumer's choice and quality of future goods of services.

It would certainly be hazardous to advance the existence of an abuse as defined by both Article 101 and Article 102 TFEU for making "the conclusion of contracts subject to acceptance by the other parties of supplementary obligations which, by their nature or according to commercial usage, have no connection with the subject of such contracts", where the conclusion of the contract between the consumer and the financial institution would be subject to the supplementary obligation of passing the information to a credit bureau. Too much controversy would exist over the locutions in the provision 'nature' or the 'commercial usage' or 'having no connection'. Traditional economic theory, debatable as it may be, would not allow to even come close to such a suggestion.

Nevertheless, it looks undeniable that an indirect form of tying exists even if not caught by traditional competition law and its cases. In the own judgement of the financial services industry and by its own rules, such tying practice may give benefits to consumers but it may also cause them harm. For the good or the bad, it will determine future consumer choices.

As said, this argument would find no support in the economic thinking of competition law and it may not have direct relevance for black-letter competition law itself, but it nevertheless reiterates questions over the market power of credit bureaus on consumers, whose market behaviour will be determined in a way or the

---

[77] In the EU no proprietary rights exist on information but the rights granted by data protection law.

other by the centralised database organised and managed by commercial organisations not acting for defined or accepted prevailing policy goals.

For competition economists and traditional lawyers the suggestion that competition law should take this aspect into account is most probably a blasphemy.

But at some point it will have to be questioned for how long competition law may be entitled to live in a box legitimatising or supporting abnormal outcomes on other fronts, or just liquidating such matters as regulatory failures at other levels or for the competence of other areas of law to adjust. For example, being the repository of all consumer information would make any organisation very powerful, not only commercially. How much economic, social and political power is society ready to concede to a dominant commercial entity is a question that sooner or later policy makers will have to come to terms with. This is of course a matter of liberty, not strict competition law.

But it questions whether or to what extent traditional competition law is suitable to host markets with features that exceed pure economic analysis inherent in interpreting its rules.

In other industries, such as utilities, telecoms, transports, etc. competition policy has played the role of breaking down monopolies and power, attempting to increase efficiency.

More modestly, here some of the problems underlined in this section would be at least addressed if the exchange of information occurred in the pursue of defined policy goals in the public interest, ideally under the rule of law.

4.11   Concluding Remarks

The EU has an underdeveloped information structure which differs from Member State to Member State. If on the one hand this jeopardised picture originates from a traditional fragmentation of the underlying retail financial markets, on the other hand it constitutes a barrier in itself for the integration of EU credit markets for consumers. The different legal forms of the information providers, the type and amount of data to be exchange, and overall the absence of a uniform or harmonised set of norms, are key factors responsible for such a poor integration.

Thus, although the EU has enacted legislation in the areas of consumer credit and mortgage lending requiring financial institutions to consult credit databases and to have cross-border access to these databases, too many obstacles exist which have the contrary effect of maintaining lending to consumers a national affair.

Non-discriminatory access is meant to promote competition at EU level. In this regard, the exchange of information may have pro-competitive effects and favour integration, but this is limited to the market entry of foreign lenders into a national system.

However, all other aspects of market integration such as the cross-border provision or reception of services, consumption in another Member State of European consumers, or access to products and services in the context of free movement of people within the EU are not served. Worse, if any, the current fragmentation poses a barrier to the exercise of the free movement established rights of the EU.

Clearly, there seem to be regulatory failures at EU level. But competition policy and law cannot be oblivious that in the EU competition is no longer an end in itself but a means to serve the internal market and its integration.

In this regard, the case law and guidelines of the European competition authorities not only represent a missed opportunity to correct the functioning of the European retail credit market, but also they risk legitimising or reinforcing an unsatisfactory status quo.

Among the many criticisms that the *Asnef* case and the *2011 Guidelines* may attract, their main limit is that they focus on the legitimacy of exchanging information, directly or indirectly, through a common third party agency but they concentrate exclusively on the assessment of the horizontal competition among lenders. In so doing, they take a narrow view of the goals of competition policy and law.

Moreover, it is argued that a major failure is represented by neglecting the information market itself. A closer look of the information infrastructure of retail financial markets reveals that this is a relevant market in itself potentially posing problems of vertical integration new vis-à-vis traditional hub-and-spoke agreements, as well as possible problems of market concentration and information monopolies which will hardly favour the integration of both EU markets in finance for consumers and in the provision of information.

What clearly appears is that the fragmentation of the information markets and the various national arrangements reflecting the legal form of providers and the type of information exchanged pose problems of system interoperability that constitute practical impediments to competition and market integration.

References

Bouckaert JH, Degryse H (2004) Softening competition by inducing switching in credit markets. J Indus Econ 52:27–52

Bouckaert JH, Degryse H (2006) Entry and strategic information display in credit markets. Econ J 116:702–720

Buch CM (2000) Information or regulation: what is driving the international activities of commercial banks? Kiel working paper no. 1011, Kiel, Kiel Institut of World Economics, November 2000

Carletti E, Vives X (2009) Regulation and competition policy in the banking sector. In: Vives X (ed) Fifty years of the treaty of Rome: assessment and perspectives of competition policy in Europe, Oxford University Press, Oxford

CEPS-ECRI (2013) Towards better use of credit reporting in Europe, CEPS-ECRI task force report, Brussels, Centre for European Policy Studies and European Credit Research Institute, September 2013

Coates K (2011) Competition law and regulation of technology markets. Oxford University Press, Oxford

Crook J (2003) The demand and supply of household debt: a cross-country comparison, working paper, European university institute workshop 'the economics of consumer credit: European experience and lessons from the U.S.', Florence, European University Institute, May 2003

Deutsche Bundesbank (2005) EU central banks open their registers for the cross-border exchange of information on loans to enterprises, press release (Frankfurt am Main). https://www.bundesbank.de/Redaktion/EN/Downloads/Press/Pressenotizen/2005/2005_06_07_credit_registers.pdf?__blob=publicationFile. Accessed 7 June 2005

Diez Guardia N (2002) Consumer credit in the European union, ECRI research report no. 1, Brussels, European Credit Research Institute 2002

European Commission (2009) Report of the expert group on credit histories , Brussels, May 2009

Fatur A (2011) EU competition law and the information and communication technology network industries. Hart Publishing, Oxford

Gehrig T, Stenbacka R (2007) Information sharing and lending market competition with switching costs and poaching. Euro Econ Rev 51:77–99

Giannetti C, Jentzsch N, Spagnolo G (2010) Information-sharing and cross-border entry in european banking, ECRI research report no. 11, Brussels, European Credit Research Institute, February 2010

Graef I (2014) How can software interoperability be achieved under European competition law and related regimes? J Eur Competition Law Prac 5(1):6–19

Graham C (2010) EU and UK competition law. Pearson Education, Harlow

Guiso L (2003) Consumer credit and household loan markets across italian regions, working paper, European university institute workshop 'the economics of consumer credit: European experience and lessons from the U.S.', Florence, European University Institute, May 2003

Jappelli T, Pagano M (2006) The role and effects of credit information Sharing. In: Bertola G, Disney R, and Grant C (eds) The economics of consumer credit, MIT Press, Cambridge, pp 347–371

Jentzsch N (2003) The regulation of financial privacy: the United States vs europe, ECRI research report no. 5, Brussels, European Credit Research Institute 2003

Jentzsch N (2006) The economics and regulation of financial privacy. Physica-Verlag, Heidelberg

Jentzsch N, San José Riestra A (2003) Information sharing and its implications for consumer credit markets: United States vs. Europe, working paper, European university institute workshop 'the economics of consumer credit: European experience and lessons from the U.S.', Florence, European University Institute, May 2003

Jentzsch N, San José Riestra A (2006) Consumer credit markets in the United States and Europe. In: Bertola G, Disney R, and Grant C (eds) The economics of consumer credit, MIT Press, Cambridge, pp 27–62

Kuneva M (2009) European consumer commissioner, keynote speech, roundtable on online data collection, targeting and profiling (Brussels). http://europa.eu/rapid/press-release_SPEECH-09-156_en.htm. Accessed 31 March 2009

Lanoo K, de la Mata Muñoz A (2004) Integration of the EU consumer credit market—proposal for a more efficient regulatory model, CEPS working document no. 213, Brussels, Centre for European Policy Studies, November 2004

Lea S, Webley P, Walker CM (1995) Psychological factors in consumer debt: money management, economic socialisation, and credit use. J Econ Psychol 16(4):681–701

Lista A (2013) EU competition law and the financial services sector. Informa Law from Routledge, London

Lorenz M (2013) An introduction to EU competition law. Cambridge University Press, Cambridge

Lyons B (2003) Introduction: the transformation of competition policy in Europe. In: Lyons B (ed) European competition policy—the economic analysis, Cambridge University Press, Cambridge, pp 1–26

Moussis N (2013) Access to European union. law, economics, policies. Intersentia, Cambridge

O'Donoghue R, Padilla J (2013) The law and economics of article 102 TFEU. Hart Publishing, Oxford

Odudu O (2011) Indirect information exchange: the constituent elements of hub and spoke collusion. Eur Competition J 7(2):205–242

Olegario R (2003) Credit reporting agencies: a historical perspective. In: Miller MJ (ed) Reporting systems and the international economy, MIT Press, Cambridge, pp 115–159

Pagano M, Jappelli T (1993) Information sharing in credit markets. J Finance 48:1693–1718

Riestra ASJ (2002) Credit bureaus in today's credit markets, ECRI research report no. 4, Brussels, European Credit Research Institute, September 2002

Rohlfs J (1974) A theory of independent demand for a communications service. Bell J Econ 5(1):16–37

Schellingerhout R (2011) Standard-setting from a competition law perspective, vol 1. Competition policy newsletter, pp 3–9

Weill L (2004) Efficiency of consumer credit companies in the European union—a cross-country frontier analysis, ECRI research report no. 7, Brussels, European Credit Research Institute, 2004

Whish R (2012) Competition law. Oxford University Press, Oxford

Wyman MO (2005) Consumer credit in Europe: riding the wave, research report, Brussels, European Credit Research Institute, November 2005

Chapter 5
Competition, the Consumer Interest, and Data Protection

5.1 Introduction: Competition Policy, Law, and the Consumer Interest

The goals and role of competition law have been a recurrent theme underlying the previous chapters, which have mostly emphasised their importance attributed in the EU as a mechanism to integrate European markets, and create or preserve the EU single market.

The maintenance of economic freedom and the promotion of economic efficiency as a means of enhancing consumer welfare have also been noted as core objectives of competition policy stirring competition law enforcement in the EU.

The concern for the consumer and his/her welfare is referenced directly in Articles 101 and 102 TFEU in terms of 'fair share of the consumer' and 'prejudice of consumers' respectively. Also, the rhetoric of making the interest of consumers, or to make markets working for consumers, figure as a constant feature in the competition law enforcement of the European authorities.

However, what accounts as the 'consumer interest' or 'welfare' remains a controversial debate, especially when other public policies or non-economic goals come into play.

It is doubtless that in most occasions the consumer interest is purely an economic concept for competition policy, and it is translated in lower prices or other economic efficiencies or benefits for consumers. Indeed, the main declared focus of competition policy is economic efficiency, even if disputes exist on how to

© The Author(s) 2014

F. Ferretti, *EU Competition Law, the Consumer Interest and Data Protection*,
SpringerBriefs in Law, DOI 10.1007/978-3-319-08906-5_5

express such efficiency, e.g. as a maximisation of total welfare for society, a redistribution of wealth, or else.[1]

At the same time, if on the one hand the concern for consumer welfare has been taken from economic thinking, on the other hand it is increasingly recognised that EU competition law is not exclusively concerned with an economic conception of the consumer interest.[2]

Monti explains that historically EU competition law has not been affected by economic paradigms as it was the case under the Chicago School-influenced antitrust law in the US. In the EU, by contrast, from a political perspective the goals of competition policy were never purely economic. At the same time, the author illustrates how whilst the European Commission has embraced the idea of consumer welfare as the benchmark for testing the legal compliance of firms, it has also become committed to avoid using non-economic considerations in the application of competition law, rejecting its use to achieve other public policy objectives, with the notable exception of market integration.[3] Following to the decentralisation operated by Regulation 1/2003 assigning EU competition law enforcement to national authorities, the policy documents issued by the European Commission for a consistent and economically sound application of the rules were clear that economic arguments should not be balanced vis-à-vis other public policy arguments carrying non-economic interests.[4]

This stance departed radically from the previous EC policy oriented at helping to attain or balance other Community objectives,[5] and it was instated in the economically buoyant years preceding the great economic crisis of the late 2000s that were largely dominated by neo-liberal ideology.

Most probably, the pursuit or consideration for other non-economic goals under competition law is at odds with neo-liberalism.

However, as it has been noted by others, the great economic crisis has forced most areas of economic and regulatory policy into a period of pressure to return to a modified version of the public interest and to rethink outcomes, driving authorities to be more mindful of wider social goals.[6]

---

[1] MacCulloch (2010), pp. 77–106; Monti (2007), Andriychuk (2009), pp. 77–87; Cseres (2007).

[2] Ibid. See also Buttigieg (2009), Amato (1997).

[3] Monti (2007).

[4] European Commission's Notice concerning agreements, decisions and concerted practices in the field of co-operation between enterprises, OJ 1968, C 75/3, replaced by the Commission's Guidelines on the applicability of Article 81 to horizontal co-operation agreements, OJ 2001, C 3/2, in turn replaced by the Commission's Guidelines on the applicability of Article 101 of the Treaty on the Functioning of the European Union to horizontal co-operation agreements, OJ 2011, C 1/25.

[5] Whish (2012).

[6] Evans (2012), pp. 545–564; Townley (2009).

Moreover, the adoption of the Treaty of Lisbon has brought significant policy developments towards a social market economy and the promotion of fundamental rights.[7]

A novelty of the Treaty of Lisbon is that, contrary to its predecessors, it no longer includes competition among its goals.

This omission has divided commentators as to the implications when other policies are at stake. Some scholarship has deducted that the absence of competition policy in the declared objectives of the EU in Article 3 TEU means that the European Commission, the CJEU, and national competition authorities now have a wider scope to include non-economic interests and other policy goal in competition cases.[8]

Others, on the contrary, find this argument unconvincing or overestimating because competition policy is nonetheless included as a Union competence in Article 3(1)(b) TFEU. Also, the fact that Protocol 27 of the TFEU declares that the internal market includes a system in which competition is not distorted prompts to the conclusion there is no effective difference between the situation before and after the enactment of the Treaty of Lisbon.[9] After all, in the *TeliaSonera* case the CJEU confirmed this perception making express reference to Protocol 27.[10]

However, there seems to be a decisive element in the Treaty of Lisbon that persuades to maintain that non-economic considerations should be part of competition law analysis and enforcement. This is the consolidation and reinforcement done by the Treaty of Lisbon of the so-called 'policy-linking clauses' which make sure that the EU grants consistency between its different policies and activities, taking all of the Union's objectives into account.[11]

Accordingly, therefore, there seem to be increasing agreement that competition policy and law cannot—and should not—be based solely on economic theory. While economic efficiency remains a perfectly legitimate goal of competition law,

---

[7] Union objectives now explicitly include a social market economy. Article 3 TEU explicitly provides for a "sustainable development of Europe based on (…) a highly competitive social market economy (…). See also the social rights in the Charter of Fundamental Rights of the European Union annexed to the Treaty of Lisbon. Significantly, the Charter elevates consumer protection and personal data protection to the status of fundamental rights. See respectively Article 38 and Article 8 of the Charter. Finally, see Article 169 TFEU (ex Article 153 TEC) which states that "in order to promote the interests of consumers and to ensure a high level of consumer protection, the Union shall contribute to protecting the health, safety and economic interests of consumers, as well as to promoting their right to information, education and to organise themselves in order to safeguard their interests".

[8] Riley (2007), Weitbrecht (2008), pp. 81–88; Petit and Neyrinck (2010), pp. 1–14; Townley (2009), Townley (2011), pp. 441–448; Parret (2009–2010), pp. 1–48.

[9] Lavrijssen (2010), pp. 636–659; O'Donoghue and Padilla (2013).

[10] *Konkurrensverket v TeliaSonera Sverige AB* (Case C-52/09) ECR I-527, paras 20–22.

[11] Article 7 TFEU.

it is not the only objective, and in the event of conflict or intersection between different objectives or non-economic interests a more balanced approach should be taken towards the central goals of the EU as expressed in the Treaty.[12]

Indeed, new scholarship has started to investigate more closely the relationship between competition law and consumer law. Despite noting the traditional focus on the regulation of the market process in general under competition law vis-à-vis the regulation of the specific transaction between businesses and consumers under consumer law, as well as the resulting different nature assigned to consumers under the two disciplines, bridging or converging concepts have emerged in the analysis of EU law.[13] In addition, the integration in many Member States of the competition authorities with their consumer protection agencies points to a convergence or the advancement of substantive competition and consumer law enforcement. Increasing complementarities between the two are emerging beside the traditional tensions.

These developments and the new impetus of the Treaty of Lisbon may thus probably test the once sensible argument that "using competition law to supplement consumer protection legislation is a misuse of powers" by the EU.[14] On this occasion, however, the term 'complement' would probably be more suitable.

The following sections, therefore, will look at the issue of competition and financial information in light of these developments, bearing in mind that *Asnef*— but not the *2011 Guidelines*—preceded the Treaty of Lisbon.

However, since personal data are involved, the new challenge could be represented by the effects of fundamental rights on competition law. The case at study, in fact, tests probably for the first time the intersection of consumer fundamental rights vis-à-vis the consumer interest and it intrudes on the inclusion of other goals for competition law analysis and enforcement.

5.2 The Consumer of Financial Services in the Decision of the CJEU and in the Guidelines of the European Commission

As noted, Article 101(3) TFEU exempts from the prohibition set forth in Article 101(1) when the benefits resulting from a concerted practice outweigh its distortive effects, particularly on those occasions where it improves the production or distribution of goods or promotes technical or economic progress, at the same time allowing consumers a fair share of the resulting benefit.

---

[12] Lavrijssen (2010), pp. 636–659; Townley (2009); Monti (2002), pp. 1057–1099; Andriychuk (2009), pp. 77–87; de Vries (2013), pp. 169–192. *Contra* see Odudu (2010), pp. 599–613.

[13] MacCulloch (2010), pp. 77–106; Haracoglou (2007), pp. 175–208; Monti (2007), Albors-Llorens (2006), pp. 245–270.

[14] Monti (2007), sp. 102.

The justification for this legal exception is that an aim of EU completion law is the protection of competition to enhance consumer welfare and ensure the optimal allocation of resources in the marketplace, thus making it necessary to balance possible efficiency gains vis-à-vis anticompetitive effects and assess the net effect of an agreement or concerted practice.

In *Asnef*, the CJEU ruled that if the referring court finds that there is a restriction of competition in the information exchange under the criteria set in the first part of the ruling, then it is necessary to conduct an assessment under the exception provided in Article 101(3) and its four cumulative conditions.

In the assessment of the 'fair share' of the profit for consumers, the CJEU established that credit bureaus "are capable of helping to prevent situations of overindebtedness for consumers" and overall lead to a greater availability of credit and favour the mobility of consumers.[15]

Once more, the CJEU starting point appears vitiated by the failure to distinguish between public institutions and private companies and their function in the economy and society, including failure to the question as to who entrusted commercial companies with a public or social function, and the type and amount of information necessary to achieve that goal.

Similarly, for the reasons first explained above in Chap. 2 and 3 of this work, the reference to the greater mobility of consumers signifies that the CJEU had in mind national markets and not the EU internal market. On the contrary, as it has been noted, a major problem of the exchange of consumer financial information is that it hampers the mobility of European consumers.

In addition, by depicting all such virtues of commercial bureaus, the CJEU puts into question how certain jurisdictions such as those without commercial credit bureaus could cope without them.

Ultimately, however, what raises most doubts in the assessment of Article 101(3) TFEU is the conclusion that the claimed economic advantages might be such as to offset the disadvantages of a possible restriction on competition, leaving it to national courts to verify that.[16]

Likewise, in the *2011 Guidelines* the European Commission regards the exchange of consumer data in markets with asymmetric information about consumers as giving raise to efficiencies. The example put forward is precisely that of keeping track of the past behaviour of customers in terms of credit defaults, providing an incentive for customers to limit their risk exposure and making it possible to detect consumers with a lower risk, who should ultimately benefit from lower prices. In the view of the European Commission, such an information exchange can also reduce consumer lock-in because consumers could benefit from otherwise exclusionary information when switching to another competing financial institution.[17] So, according to the reasoning of the European Commission, the

---

[15] *Asnef*, para 67.

[16] Ibid.

[17] See *2011 Guidelines*, para 97, sp. 21.

competing institution would be prone to accept a customer for the information supplied by the competitor, de facto influencing the former. Note that the European Commission stresses the positive benefit of a consumer who clearly has a credit history and it is positive. It tactfully or neglectfully omits the scenario of the competitor *declining* the customer because of negative information who will remain locked-in.

At least, the CJEU admits that, owing to the existence of credit bureaus, certain consumers will be faced with increased interest rates or be refused credit. However, in the CJEU view the fact that some consumers will pay more or are refused credit cannot prevent the condition that consumers are allowed a fair share of the benefit.[18]

The latter assessment is problematic for the determination of the type of consumer targeted by the European authorities, especially since this is not a statistical test but it should depend on many contextual factors.[19]

At any rate, the problem is that such consumers who are refused credit or pay more are those usually identified as the 'vulnerable consumers',[20] including over-indebted people, who will have worse conditions or be economically and socially excluded.[21] Nonetheless, disregarding any possible social concern or regard for minorities, the CJEU is of the view that under Article 101(3) it is the beneficial nature of the effect on *all consumers* in the relevant markets that must be taken into consideration, not the effect on each member of that category of consumers.[22] Under the debatable assumption that credit bureaus are capable of leading to a greater availability of credit, they become beneficial for applicants whom interest rates might be higher if lenders did not know of their personal situation as portrayed by credit data.[23]

Clearly, this view denies the value of traditional market intelligence, where those who are better at really knowing their clients are able to offer better deals and lower prices, thus prevailing over inefficient competitors.

Probably, it could be also argued that it over-estimates the use of credit data or at least puts a shadow over other methods of better knowing customers and assessing contractual risks. The unsaid reality may be that it is more profitable for lenders to screen customers *en masse* with automated tools rather than one-by-one,

---

[18] *Asnef*, para 69.

[19] See Recital 18 of Directive 2005/29/EC OJ L 149/22 of 11.06.2005 (Unfair Commercial Practices Directive); see also Ramsay (2012), sp. Ch. 4.

[20] Cartwright (2011), Cartwright (2010), sp. 205–226.

[21] According to the latest definitions, vulnerable consumers are over-indebted people, the migrants, the unemployed or people on low or irregular incomes, elderly people or pensioners, disable people, prisoners or ex-prisoners. See European Foundation for Financial Inclusion (2013). On the latest academic account on consumer vulnerability see Waddington (2013), pp. 757–782.

[22] *Asnef*, para 70.

[23] *Asnef*, para 71.

which *inter alia* contradicts—instead of promoting—best practices of risk management and responsible lending.

But how much of this profit is passed on to consumers cannot be known, and it nevertheless remains questionable to what extent they make a greater availability of credit. Moreover, the examples of France and Belgium, where no such databases exist in the form considered, appear to contradict this assumption. The great economic crisis of the late 2000s and the following credit crunch demonstrate that the availability of credit data is probably not such an important factor in credit provisioning or rationing, or at least it would not be easy to explain why despite a greater availability of data than ever financial institutions have stopped lending during and in the aftermath of the crisis. This goes far beyond this study, but certain economic assumptions put forward by the judiciary and the European Commission may seem too biased and probably out of place.

In any case, it remains open the non-negligible issue of the type or image of consumers that the Court and the European Commission had and have in mind when affirming that consumers enjoy the fair share of the alleged benefit.

5.3   The *Homo Economicus* Under Competition Law: Going Beyond the 'Average' and the 'Vulnerable' Consumer

Indeed, the main question that arises from the case-law and the *2011 Guidelines* is the determination of the type of consumer under competition law in the financial sector.

Finance, in fact, is a delicate sector for the far-reaching consequences it may have on the many facets of the lives of people, not only present but also future.

The importance of such determination lies in the understanding of the 'interest' that regulation pursues or the 'harm' of anti-competitive practices, which become particularly relevant under competition law.[24]

Making the interest or protecting consumers broadly, in fact, is one of the greatest challenges for regulation. This is because, as it is well known, consumers are a very heterogeneous group: they dispose of different economic assets or incomes, they may be educated at very different levels, they belong to very broad age groups, they are of different gender and ethnicity, they have different levels of trust or rationality patterns, different values, attitudes and decision-making behaviour, and so on and so forth.[25]

Within such a wide and diverse group, it is hard to find a one-fit-all common denominator for the consumer as the beneficiary of regulation.

---

[24]   See Article 101(3) and Article 102 TFEU.

[25]   E.g. see Wilhelmsson (2006), pp. 123–165.

The search for an appropriate image of the consumer who is the addressee of regulation is a recurring theme in the study of law, especially consumer law. In this perspective, legal scholarship has devoted abundant efforts and produced many analyses.[26]

This is not the right place to retrieve all the debates on the conceptions of the consumer in EU law and their critique. Overall, however, a common thread is that of acknowledging the existence of an imbalance when consumers deal with businesses that makes the former the weaker party of the relationship.

But note is taken that under the jurisprudence of the CJEU the dominant concept under EU law has developed from 'the average consumer', portraying a somehow robust model of a consumer who is 'reasonably well informed and reasonably observant and circumspect'.[27] Such view has mostly reflected an initial need of the EU judiciary to lift existing national laws protecting national trade but camouflaged under consumer protection that obstructed European integration, applying the test of the possible harmful effect on consumers following the removal of such protectionist laws.[28] However, over time, in a quest for legitimacy and under political pressure,[29] this image of the reasonably informed, observant, and circumspect consumer has been balanced with the need to recognise social, cultural, and linguistic interests and protect the weaker or vulnerable consumer.[30]

Generally, therefore, the difficult determination a priori of who is the consumer to be protected or in whose interest a norm provides, as well as the assessment of the many circumstances that need to be looked at contextually, all have induced scholarship to agree on the open texture of the concept of 'average' and the importance of 'vulnerability'.[31]

Realising how complex the concept of consumer is and the corresponding difficult task of interpreting and applying the law, coupled with the sensitivity of the consumer financial sector, it is unclear why a proper assessment of the consumer of finance did not become the object of the competition law analysis of both the CJEU and the European Commission. On the contrary, the treatment of the concept as described in the Section above induces caution.

A problem under competition law and its economic analysis may lie in the neoclassical understanding or bias of the consumer as purely a *homo economicus*.

---

[26] See, for example, MacCulloch (2010), pp. 77–106; Weatherill (2007), pp. 115–138; Cartwright (2011), Wilhelmsson (2004), pp. 317–337; Wilhelmsson (2007), pp. 1–21; Waddington (2013), pp. 757–782.

[27] *Gut Springenheide and Tusky v Oberkreisdirektordes Kreises Steinfurt* (Case C-210/96) [1998] ECR I-4657; see also *Verein gegen Unwesen In Handel und Gewerbe Köln eV v. Mars GmbH* (Case C-470/93) [1995] ECR 1-1923.

[28] Weatherill (2007), pp. 1–21.

[29] Micklitz (2006), pp. 83–121.

[30] *Estée Lauder Cosmetics GmbH & Co OHG v Lancaster Group GmbH* (Case C-220/98) [2000] ECR I-117; *R Buet and Educational Business Services (EBS) v Ministère public* (Case 382/87) [1989] ECR-1235.

[31] Ramsay (2012), Waddington (2013), pp. 757–782.

Despite the recognition that the exchange of information can cause severe damage to some consumers, the current economic analysis and judicial interpretation envision a consumer who is perfectly rational, vigilant and alert, who knows how the information exchange works, who understands the value and meaning given to information, who appreciates its association with other information, who regularly identifies and disputes errors, etc. In short, the economic behaviour of consumers is explained as if they were fully rational, narrowly self-interested actors who have the ability to make judgments towards their subjectively defined ends; consumers who maximise their own utility and make intelligent choices, free of external events biasing their behaviour.[32]

Such an economic regulatory approach and interpretation is inconsistent with the increasing acceptance in consumer policy of the behavioural literature, which has guided policy makers and Courts elsewhere in the framing of commercial practices and the correspondent assessment of the average consumer and the vulnerability of different groups.[33]

By contrast, behavioural economics attempts to explain relevant features of human behaviour and the consumers' cognitive limitations that cannot be explained under standard economic assumptions. It challenges economic assumptions by using a number of alternative social sciences or disciplines such as psychology, sociology, neurosciences to explore the real behaviour of human beings and how economic decisions are taken in the economic, cultural, and social context where they live.[34]

To the extent that behavioural economics is closer to human reality and it more appropriately informs policies and judgements in consumer law, it is hard to understand, and difficult to accept, why the same judiciary and policy makers employ different standards when it comes to competition law enforcement.

MacCulloch explains it as the situation when two 'families' of lawyers use the same terminology but in a completely different way. Competition policy and law is a servant of the economy and in its enforcement the consumer's importance is not linked to the intrinsic nature of the consumer.[35]

Cseres, in turn, stresses that in competition law the primary role of the consumer welfare standard is to verify the goals of competition policy, i.e. economic efficiency. In consumer law, by contrast, the consumer welfare is measured by the correction of market failures to improve the position of the consumer in market transactions.[36]

---

[32] Staten and Cate (2004), Becker (1976), Osovsky (2013), pp. 881–933.

[33] Ramsay (2012).

[34] The literature on behavioural economics is copious. Examples are Jolls et al. (1998), pp. 1471–1550; Diamond and Vartiainen (2007), Camerer et al. (2003), pp. 1211–1254; Hansen and Kysar (1999), pp. 630–749.

[35] MacCulloch (2010), pp. 77–106.

[36] Cseres (2007), pp. 121–173.

At any rate, whatever the explanations and as realistic as these may be, the unsatisfactory outcome of the different conception of the consumer remains palpable, not only for the inconsistencies that it leads to but also for the integrity of the legal system as a whole.

In the case at hand, it looks that neither the average nor the vulnerable consumers are accounted.

Arguably, the dismissal of the effects on vulnerable consumers is worrying per se. Moreover, in *Asnef* the CJEU is not concerned to investigate why consumers may not have repaid certain debts or paid them late but nevertheless repaid (adding additional interest rates to the repayment). As already noted, life time events such as illness, divorce, job losses, etc. and/or poor market conditions in the economy are the major causes of consumer failure to repay debts timely or over-indebtedness.[37] These situations cannot be caught or resolved by credit data and their exchange. All what data do is that they represent outcomes of possibly unique or circumstantiated situations coldly without distinguishing the causes, and they retrieve and give a memory to such representations that become accessible to all other market players, thus *inter alia* raising doubts as to their ability to predict whether the same consumer will repay loaned money in the absence of those lifetime events that once originated the data themselves.

Arguably, giving a second chance to consumers may well be in the consumer interest and it may even be economically efficient. Wouldn't the consumer interest be better satisfied if a proper assessment of the applicant financial situation is undertaken without reliance on an exchange of information that presents a partial or fragmented story or situation?

Additional questions arise: what about those who are not in the databases? Why should they be left out by the interpretation of the Court regarding the consumer interest? Arguably, those who are not in the databases for not having incurred into any financing operation are not negligible in numbers. They are not even vulnerable consumers or, more appropriately, consumers in a current position of vulnerability.

Rather, the impression is that the consumer that the CJEU had in mind is a new 'elitist consumer', forming in itself a category of consumers, who is prone to making debts and has developed a financial CV, with an immaculate credit history and absence of problems beyond the unwillingness to repay a debt. Or, putting it differently, it is the ideal consumer for the financial industry, i.e. elitist not for his/her own merits or achievements, but for being as profitable for the industry as the latter wants him/her to be. It is a consumer shaped by the industry who behaves according to its standards and who needs to develop his/her credit history in a way marked by it as a gateway to other goods or services (e.g. credit cards, the best mortgage or other credit deals, favourable telecom contracts, etc.).

---

[37] Ramsay (2007), sp. 578–580; Caplovitz (1963), Adler and Wozniak (1980), Berthoud and Kempson (1992), Hoermann (1986), Elliott (2005), Balmer et al. (2006), pp. 39–51; Dominy and Kempson (2003).

They are consumers who have not fallen victim to family breakings; they are healthy and skilled, or even lucky enough to resist economic downturns, better if without too many family members at his/her dependency, etc. This is of course a caricature and a picture voluntary stretched. But a more down to earth portray nonetheless shows a disconnection between the economic consumer under the competition law enforcement of the CJEU and the European Commission with a broader social reality and possible problems. Most certainly, the current image given to the consumer disregards the protection of the vulnerable members of society, bearing in mind that this is an open category of consumers where any person may fall in any time in life.

If the consumer interest lies at the heart of competition policy, and the maximisation of consumer welfare features prominently among its goals, the idea that 'all consumers' coincide with those best placed in society or, in an extreme portray, 'those best placed as customers for the financial industry', but who may become vulnerable at any time, may be undesirable and set a dangerous precedent.

Moreover, because competition law is in large part designed to promote markets which work for consumers and serve their interest, the concept of who is the consumer and what their interest is needs to be broader and more inclusive, especially in a delicate area such as the financial one. Indeed, substantial parts of European consumer law are designed precisely to deal with situations where markets do not function fairly even when they may work efficiently, embracing the concept of consumer protection especially in the area of financial services.[38]

Once more, thus, one may assert that regulatory failures emerge at various levels before competition law enforcement.

At the same time, that policy makers and the judiciary employ double standards not the same in every situation remains an unclear assessment which leads to the undesirable outcome of competition law standing isolated in its own dimension and giving legitimacy to practices that may be harmful on other grounds.

The suspicion is that the current strict economic analysis of competition law and the economic consumer are better positioned to serve corporate interests.

5.4   Data Protection Law

5.4.1   Understanding the Concept and Value of Data Protection

Data protection is a complex and multifaceted concept both from a social and a legal point of view. Traditionally, it has been identified with the protection of personal privacy within the context of processing operations involving personal

---

[38] For example, see generally Micklitz (ed.) (2011). See also Micklitz (2011), pp. 3–60; Benöhr and Micklitz (2010) pp. 19–47; Micklitz (2013), pp. 18–47.

data. However, at least under EU law, the two are distinct, yet complementary, fundamental legal rights. They derive their normative force from values that, although at times coincidental and interacting in a variety of ways, may be conceptualised independently.

Even though the recognition of the idea of privacy is deeply rooted in history,[39] its concept has been seen as always in transition.[40] It was first developed as an independent legal value when Brandeis and Warren identified it as a tort action, defining it as 'the right to be left alone'.[41] Since then, it has been largely accepted that in its most general accession, privacy protection is a legal way of drawing a line at how far society or other individual subjects may intrude into a person's own affairs. It entails that such a person should be left able to conduct their personal legitimate affairs relatively free from unwanted intrusions. As such, privacy is an expression of human dignity, development of human personality, and individual freedom.[42]

However, modern ideas of privacy have been first tested, then shaped, by innovation and the fast development of information technologies and electronic data usage in the last few decades. Today the world cannot be imagined without information technologies but with the developments and opportunities it emerged the need for new standards that allowed individuals to exercise control over their personal information while permitting innovation and that flow of information necessary to support international trade, business, enhanced security and so on. In practice, there is an unprecedented scale of personal data stored on the internet and used for commercial purposes. Information processing and technologies have a clear potential to influence dramatically the lives of people and this provides an exceptional power in the hands of those who use them, a risk only recently perceived by business and consumer associations alike.[43] Thus, after the landmark definition by Warren and Brandeis other definitions have followed, from the right to control how others use personal information[44] to the vindication of the

---

[39] Electronic Privacy Information Center and Privacy International (2002).

[40] Jay and Hamilton (2003), MacDonald (2000), pp. 54–75.

[41] Warren and Brandeis (1890), pp. 193–220.

[42] See, for example, Bloustein (1964), pp. 962–1007: Stromholm (1967), Pennock and Chapman (1971), Paul et al. (2000), Rachels (1975), pp. 323–333. Other narrower views of privacy see it as self-determination, intimacy, or a meaningful aspect of interpersonal relationships, personal expression, and choice. See, for example, Parent (1983), pp. 269–288; Gerstein et al. (1978), pp. 76–81; Westin (1967), Inness (1992), Fried (1970), Gavison (1980), pp. 421–471; Moore et al. (1998), pp. 365–378; Schoeman (1984), DeCew (1997). Such an individualistic approach to privacy has been criticised by scholarship arguing that greater recognition should be given to the broader social importance of privacy: other than a common value in which individuals enjoy some degree of it, privacy is seen as a public and collective value vis-à-vis technological developments and market forces, requiring minimal levels of privacy for all. Regan (1995).

[43] London Economics (2010).

[44] Westin (1967); see also the landmark decision of the German Constitutional Court *Bundersverfassungsgericht*, Judgement of 15 December 1983, 1 BvR 209/83, BVerfGE 65 establishing the right of informational self-determination.

boundaries protecting individuals' right not to be simplified, objectified or evaluated out of context.[45]

Indeed, data protection refers to the protection of identified or identifiable individuals (data subjects) through the regulation of personal information. Individuals do not own information about themselves. Information does not pre-exist to its expression or disclosure but it is always to some extent constructed or created by more than one agent.[46] Normatively, no copyright or proprietary rights exist on personal information. It pertains to a person but it does not belong in a proprietary sense to him/her. Those who process personal data (data controllers) have the right to process data pertaining to data subjects as long as such processing is lawful, i.e. they abide by procedural rules set by a law whose objective is to protect individual citizens not against data processing per se but against unjustified collection, storage, use, and dissemination of the data pertaining to them.[47]

As persuasively shown by De Hert and Gutwirth, data protection cannot be reduced to a late privacy spin-off echoing a privacy right with regard to personal data, but it formulates the conditions under which information processing is legitimate. While privacy laws derive their normative force from the need to protect the legitimate opacity of the individual through prohibitive measures, data protection forces the transparency of the processing of personal data enabling its full control by the data subjects where the processing is not authorised by the law itself as necessary for societal reasons. In short, data protection law focuses on the activities of the processors and it enforces their accountability, thus regulating an accepted exercise of power.[48]

Like privacy, therefore, data protection finds its roots in the idea that democratic societies should not be turned into societies resting on control, surveillance, actual or predictive profiling, classification, sorting, and discrimination. It is not only a matter of individual liberty, intimacy, integrity, and dignity of individuals but a wider personality right aimed at developing people's social identity as citizens and consumers alike.

Hence, it has to be agreed with those concluding that, although "data protection principles might seem less substantive and more procedural compared to other rights (...) they are in reality closely tied to substantial values and protect a broad scale of fundamental values"[49] that on many occasions may overlap or intersect but remain separate from those of privacy. For that reason, it also has important connotations for society as a whole and it constitutes an important legislative tool to protect a collective social good and fundamental value of a modern democratic

---

[45] Rosen (2000).

[46] Rouvroy and Poullet (2009), pp. 45–76.

[47] On discussions about individuals not owning information about themselves see Kang and Bunter (2004), pp. 230–267; Rouvroy and Poullet (2009), pp. 45–76.

[48] De Hert and Gutwirth (2009), pp. 3–44. On a critical view that data protection acts are seldom privacy laws but rather information laws, protecting data before people, see Davis (1997), pp. 143–165.

[49] De Hert and Gutwirth (2009), pp. 3–44, sp. 44.

order where citizens freely develop their personality and autonomy. Both privacy and data protection regimes—seclusion and legitimate opacity on the one side, and inclusion, participation, and transparency on the other side—represent a bundle of legal protections and tools to pursue the common goal of a free and democratic society where citizens develop their own personality freely and autonomously through individual reflexive self-determination and for collective deliberative decision making regarding the rules of social cooperation.[50]

From this perspective, granting to individuals control over their personal information is not only a tool to allow them control over the *persona* they project in society free from unreasonable or unjustified associations, manipulations, distortions, misrepresentations, alterations or constraints on their true identity. It is also a fundamental value pertaining to humans to keep and develop their personality in a manner that allows them to fully participate in society without having to conform thoughts, beliefs, behaviours or preferences to those of the majority or those set from above by the industry for commercial interest.[51] In this sense, the rights conferred by data protection legislation are participatory rights.

Yet, there is another deriving fundamental value that data protection upholds. This is the protection of both individual and public trust, which translates in trust to use new information technology safely, trust in the use of information by public and private agencies, and more narrowly trust in commercial services. Trust and system trustworthiness become the gateway to secure users willingness to depend on a society that increasingly evolves and relies on information communication technologies in the provision of new forms of governance and services. In an environment where personal data processing is used for an increasing number of purposes trust may be only generated if technologies are secure, they are under individuals' control, personal integrity is respected, and those making use of personal data are accountable. The correct use of personal data, the guarantee of their protection, and transparency become the adhesive tools to ensure that trust finds the fertile ground for its roots. In this other sense, thus, the rights conferred by data protection become heterogeneous rights which affect all aspects of human life, from political to consumer rights, as well as technological development.

Notably, both privacy and data protection qualify as distinct fundamental rights rooted in fundamental values, as it clearly emerges from the EU legal framework.

5.4.2 The EU Legal Framework

Departing from a static and negative kind of protection, such as that granted by the right to privacy in its expression as the right to respect for one's private and family life, data protection as information law establishes rules on the mechanisms to

---

[50] Rouvroy and Poullet (2009), pp. 45–76.

[51] Ibid.

process data empowering individuals to control them. In this way, individuals are allowed to affirm their personality and they can contribute to its formation and expression in a framework of transparency outside the private sphere. Those powers pertain not only to the individuals themselves but also to a public independent authority.[52]

The legal protection of personal data inevitably follows the evolving conceptual shaping of privacy, up to the point of a legal separation of the two under the Treaty of Lisbon.

The legal protection of privacy rights has a far-reaching history. Legal systems in Europe have a tradition of laws on privacy, tort, secrecy and confidentiality. Fascinating as this historical perspective may be, its study is beyond the scope of this work.[53]

Narrowing it to the roots of personal data processing, to understand in depth the fundamental nature of the right to data protection it needs to be reminded how it was the experience of totalitarian regimes in the 20th Century that pushed European nations into attaching great importance to the right to privacy in its modern form. These experiences have demonstrated how easily privacy could be abused and the extreme consequences of such violations.

Privacy was soon elevated as a human right and its standard at international level was enshrined in the 1948 Universal Declaration of Human Rights. Later, at European level, it was incorporated in the 1950 European Convention for the Protection of Human Rights and Fundamental freedoms (ECHR) under the broad protection of one's private and family life, home, and correspondence.[54]

Certainly, the horrors of recent European history and the subsequent international conventions played an important role in the development of data protection laws across Europe[55] and, ultimately, at EU level in the adoption of the Data Protection Directive. Two other factors, however, proved decisive for its enactment under the remit of the EU: (i) the progressive development in computers and information technologies together with the dangers that this could represent for individuals, transcending national affairs; and (ii) the need for the free movement of personal data within the Community to solve trade disputes arising from separate national regimes, hence the harmonisation of data protection laws of the Member States.[56] In the end, the real aims and scope of the Data Protection

---

[52] Rodotà (2009), pp. 77–82.

[53] See, for example, Banisar and Davies (1999), pp. 1–111; Schober et al. (2002), pp. 703–754.

[54] Universal Declaration of Human Rights, 10 December 1948. Council of Europe, Convention for the Protection of Human Rights and Fundamental Freedoms, ETS n. 005.

[55] For example, in 1970 the German state of *Hesse* enacted what can be considered the first known modern data protection law, which was largely motivated by the growing potential of IT systems combined with the fear of the experience of abuses that took place under the Third Reich before and during the war and the need to prevent their reoccurrence. Other European countries followed the example with similar national initiatives.

[56] See Directive 95/46/EC, OJ L 281, 23.11.1995, Recitals 1-11. A sector specific regime with regard to privacy and electronic communications was the recently amended Directive 2002/58/

Directive were both the protection of fundamental rights and freedoms of Europeans and the achievement of the internal market. Both objectives were equally important, though in mere legal terms the existence of the Directive, and the jurisdiction of the EU, rested on Internal Market grounds, having its legal basis in then Article 100a of the EC Treaty (now Article 114 TFEU).

All the same, in the drafting of the law the EU consistently took a rigorous 'fundamental human rights' approach. This stance was particularly important because it meant that data protection automatically trumped other interests and could not be traded-off for economic benefits.[57]

This position has been made explicit by the Treaty of Lisbon which in its Article 16 TFEU upgrades the provision on data protection to a 'provision of general application' under Title II alongside other fundamental principles of the EU. It also imposes on the EU legislator to establish a certain and unequivocal legal framework for data protection.

Equally, with the Treaty of Lisbon, the Charter of Fundamental Rights of the EU (the 'Charter') has become binding. Normatively, the Charter contains the two distinct rights of 'privacy' in Article 7, and the recognition of the protection of 'personal data' as an autonomous right distinguished from privacy in Article 8.

To meet the challenges of rapid technological developments and the modern economy, the European Commission has now drafted a proposal in the form of a

---

(Footnote 56 continued)

EC (the so-called 'e-Privacy Directive'), OJ 2002 L201 pp. 37–47, as amended by Directive 2009/136/EC OJ 2009 L377 pp. 11–36. It is a *lex specialis* vis-à-vis the Data Protection Directive providing for a sector specific regime exclusively applicable to providers of publicly available electronic communication services (e.g. telecom and internet service providers) with regard to the protection of personal data in electronic communications.

[57] *Rechnungshof v Osterreichischer Rundfunk and Others* (Case C-465/00) [2002] ECR I-4989. See also Heisenberg (2005), sp. Chap. 1, 2, 3; Mayer-Schonberger (1997), pp. 219–241; Simitis (1994/1995), pp. 445–469. Indeed, the draft relied heavily on the German and French data protection laws, reflecting views that data privacy could not be traded-off against commercial interests or other rights such as freedom of expression. Moreover, there was a strategic element to the choice of labelling data protection as a fundamental human right. The CJEU (ex ECJ) had ruled that it was bound by the constitutional traditions of the Member States and it could not uphold measures incompatible with fundamental rights recognised and protected by the constitutions of those states. According to the CJEU, thus, the EC could not take away the Member States' guaranteed rights, and there was therefore a legal duty not to harmonise at the lowest level in order to avoid conflicts between EC law and the Member States' Constitutions (*Internationale Handlelsgesellschaft mbH v Einfuhr—und Vorratsstelle fur Getreide und Futtermittel* (Case C-11/70) [1970] ECR 1125, [1972] CMLR 255; *Nold (J.) KG v Commission* (Case C-4/73) [1974] ECR 491, [1974] 2 CMLR 338). Not all Member States approved the described 'fundamental human rights approach' taken by Directive 95/46/EC, cit. *supra* at note n. 56. In particular, the UK sided with its business community, complaining that the new standards were much higher than the law existing at the time, mainly maintaining a utilitarian stance and disagreeing on the fact that data protection should not have been traded-off for economic benefits. Isolated in its position, the UK abstained from voting on the Directive, signalling to its business community that it had opposed its strict provisions. On the utilitarian approach of the UK, see Kenyon and Richardson (2006), 1–10.

Regulation (hereinafter 'Proposed Regulation')[58] in view to reform the current legal framework for data protection of Directive 95/46/EC.[59] The declared policy objective is to achieve consistent and effective legal implementation and application of the fundamental right to protection of personal data in all areas of the Union's activities while continuing to guarantee a high level of protection of individuals.

5.5 Data Protection and the Consumer Interest

If the traditional justification of consumer protection and law is to correct market failures and readjust the position of consumers in the market vis-à-vis businesses, social justice and the redistribution of wealth are becoming increasingly important rationales of consumer policy and law to realign the position of consumers in society.[60]

Likewise, fundamental rights of individuals are becoming a dominant component of EU law. The interaction between fundamental rights recognised by the EU and markets is not new to the literature.[61]

Nonetheless, the case at study offers a textbook exemplification where professed economic efficiency may interfere with fundamental rights.

Personal financial data are the backbone of the information exchange among competitors and its relationship with competition law. Obviously, therefore, in collecting, processing, and disseminating the personal data of consumers in financial operations, credit bureaus and lenders must, like any other European data controller, comply with data protection legislation.

In the previous section it has been stressed that EU law guarantees a high level of normative protection for data subjects and that the EU legislator has consistently taken a rigorous 'fundamental human rights' approach trumping other interests, including economic benefits.[62]

---

[58] COM (2012) 11 final of 25/1/2012, preceded by European Commission, *Communication from the Commission to the European Parliament, the Council, the Economic and Social Committee and the Committee of the Regions—A comprehensive approach on personal data protection in the European Union*, 4 November 2010, COM (210) 609 final. At the time of writing, the Proposed Regulation is under the scrutiny of the European Parliament and the Council for adoption.

[59] Directive 95/46/EC, cit. *supra* at note n. 56.

[60] Howells and Weatherill (2005), pp. 1–98; Ramsay (2012), pp. 1–82.

[61] See generally, for example, Dine and Fagan (2006); see also Benöhr and Micklitz (2010), 19–47.

[62] Heisenberg (2005), sp. Ch. 1, 2, 3; Mayer-Schonberger (1997), pp. 219–41; Simitis (1994–1995), pp. 445–469.

Even if the decision in *Asnef* precedes the Treaty of Lisbon, the Court is not oblivious of the role of data protection law but it dissociates it from competition law.

Holding that

> any possible issue relating to the sensitivity of personal data are not a matter of competition law and must be resolved on the basis of the relevant provisions governing data protection,[63]

the CJEU seems to suggest that as long as the parties involved comply with the requirements of data protection law, this is not a matter concerning competition. The Court is not interested in investigating whether information exchanges among competitors comply with requirements of data minimisation, purpose limitation, necessariety, consent, or other legitimising elements for the data exchange.[64] It gives compliance for assumed.

Yet, consumer financial data exchanged by credit bureaus are not processed for competition purposes and, arguably, could be caught by purpose limitation provisions, i.e. lenders may find it difficult to justify information sharing for competition purposes, because risk-management is the alleged processing purpose.

At any rate, the idea that a court of justice delegates such questions elsewhere because it is competition law that it is investigating shows that different areas of law are left to run in a parallel dimension even if they intersect.

At the same time, it is interesting to note that in another decision *Asnef and Fecemd versus Administración del Estado*[65] the same Court justifies the processing of negative data, not the positive ones, on grounds of the 'legitimate interest' of the credit industry, not of consumers. The processing of positive data remains on the consent of the consumer, which is imposed on them if they do not want to be refused credit and trade under the terms imposed by the financial industry.[66]

These are not trivial issues but in a broader policy context they may probably be treated as legal niceties. Indeed, it is on policy grounds that this work aspires to transfer the discussion, particularly since the EU already recognises explicitly that "the respect of private and family life and the protection of personal data are much bigger issues than just a commercial debate".[67] The position taken by the EU is that even if commercial entities use personal data to gain commercial advantage vis-à-vis users, consumer policy needs to intervene to prevent not only abusive behaviours but also commercial manipulation.[68]

---

[63] *Asnef*, para 63.

[64] See the relevant provisions of the data protection legislation in Directive 95/46/EC cit. supra at note n. 56, sp 0031–0050.

[65] *Asnef and Fecemd v Administración del Estado* (Joined cases C-468/10 and C-469/10) [2011] I-12181.

[66] This issue has been addressed in Ferretti (2007/2008), pp. 87–130.

[67] Almunia (2012).

[68] Ibid.

Yet, credit bureaus raise issues of consumer classification, sorting, standardisation of behaviours, discrimination, financial inclusion of some and exclusion of others. Overall, consumer credit data seem to drive the conforming of consumer behaviours to the economic needs of the credit industry under the market tenets of the neo-liberal ideology.[69] All these undesirable outcomes are direct consequences of profiling, which comprises any form of automated processing of personal data intended to analyse or predict economic situations or behaviours.[70]

The problem is that, at least in theory, it is not a declared task of competition policy to tackle potentially abusive commercial behaviours that become accepted in competitive markets.[71] However, as discussed above in this work, commercial entities like credit bureaus have exclusive access to personal data in the consumer credit market and could give rise to concentration concerns, which is where personal financial data may become a competition issues anytime consumers become prevented de facto from switching to other lenders or access others in a new relationship.

Whatever the answer, competition law is there for an efficient functioning of markets, which are ultimately supposed to work for consumers. But another problem is that the consumer interest is seen only as a short-term economic gain, which in the area of financial services raises the question whether this is consumer welfare or rather longer term views are necessary. However, under the current position the fact that consumer profiling is used to achieve such short-term economic benefit is irrelevant. Taking a holistic view, the question is whether economic sorting, classification, and discrimination may ever be in the consumer interest, alongside the standardisation of their economic behaviour as dictated by the industry.

It is true that pursuant to Article 169 TFEU under Title XV—Consumer Protection—explicit reference is made to the economic interest for the promotion of the consumer interest alongside their health, safety, and rights to information, education, and organisation.

Nonetheless, if in the early days the European Commission was criticised for treating the consumer benefit of Article 101(3) as a formal condition automatically satisfied if the agreement produced an immediate economic or technical benefit, robust calls and further European Commission actions have taken place for a more analytical approach to the determination of the benefit to consumers.[72]

---

[69] In particular those advanced by the Chicago School: see Bork (1993). See also Harvey (2005). On a late account on the persistence of the neoliberal ideology in financial markets see Williams (2013), pp. 15–46.

[70] Article 29 Data Protection Working Party, *Advice paper on essential elements of a definition and a provision on profiling within the EU General Data Protection Regulation* (Brussels, 13 May 2013).

[71] Almunia (2012).

[72] Albors-Llorens (2006), pp. 245–270. On the role of the consumer in EU competition law see Reich (1997), pp. 127–137; Stuyck (2000), pp. 367–400. On the maximisation of consumer welfare featuring prominently among the goals of completion law see Bishop and Walker (1999).

Looking at the case at hand, information processing and technologies have a strong potential to influence the lives of people, and this puts an extraordinary power in the hands of those who use them—a risk that has only recently been perceived by a number of stakeholders, from business to consumer organisations.[73]

Data protection finds its roots in the idea that democratic societies should not be turned into systems of power resting on control, surveillance, actual or predictive profiling, classification, social sorting and discrimination. Data protection is not only a matter of individual liberty, intimacy, and dignity of individuals but a wider personality right aimed at developing people's social identity as citizens and consumers alike. Granting to individuals control over their personal information is not only a tool to allow them control over the *persona* they project in society free from unreasonable or unjustified associations, manipulations, distortions, misrepresentations, alterations or constraints on their true identity. It is also a fundamental value pertaining to humans to keep and develop their personality in a manner that allows them to fully participate in society without having to conform thoughts, beliefs, behaviours or preferences to those of the majority or those set from above by the industry for commercial interest.[74] In this sense, the rights conferred by data protection legislation are participatory rights of informational self-determination.

Arguably, a public institution with clear policy objectives in the interest of society and operating under a clear legal framework would be better a better fit to preserve those important values of a free society.

Ultimately, therefore, this work argues that the case of information exchange among competitors in consumer financial services illustrates the need to introduce rights in the equation, particularly data protection rights to protect a long-term interest. This is an interest of society which is made of the same people that are classified as consumers when they operate in the market. These are not just labels turning individuals in a bipolar schizophrenia depending on the circumstance. Being the holder of an interest as a member of society is not incompatible with being a consumer. Actually, it should rather be the opposite.

More generally, this view supports the argument that in the financial services sector the promotion of the consumer welfare in the application of competition law is best achieved in markets that function not only efficiently but also fairly, pressing forward the proposition of a growing association between competition policy and law, consumer interests, and fundamental rights.

---

[73] London Economics (2010).

[74] Rouvroy and Poullet (2009), pp. 45–76.

5.6 The New Frontier: Data Protection and Competition Law

5.6.1 The Non-Price Dimension of Data Protection in Competition Law

The previous section has attempted to show that data protection may feature under competition law when it accounts as a long-term non-economic interest of consumers.

Yet, data protection may intersect with competition law in other ways.

In the modern economy personal data have become an economic asset increasingly valued by firms which have made them the core of their service, or which may need them to continue or set-up their business models.[75]

Still, the case at hand shows that there is a market for personal data that until now policy-makers, regulators, and the judiciary have not defined. Not only competition authorities have not yet handled cases in which personal data were used to breach competition law.[76] Also, what this work has shown is that what to date the authorities have defined are the markets of products or services which are fuelled by personal data, and they have treated them accordingly.

But a market for the personal data themselves—specifying the buyers, the sellers, the role of consumers as those to whom the data pertain, monopoly or concentration tests, etc.—has not been defined or addressed.[77]

Under competition law and the analysis of markets the above oversight looks as an anomaly. This work has already attempted to argue that also under this perspective the assessment in *Asnef* and the *2011 Guidelines* were missed opportunities. So far personal data and their legal assessment has been treated as the exclusive competence and target of data protection legislation. But to the extent that policy-makers have shown awareness of the growth in the commercial value of personal data and the expansion of their reference market, then competition law may no longer be exempted from application.

Of course, the financial information market is not an unique case of a possible nexus between competition and personal data protection. Actually, analogous views have started to raise in the context of the digital economy dominated by large internet firms. Suggestions have been put forward that data protection should be considered as a non-price dimension in the competition analysis and review of cases.[78] Isolated voices took the stance that the European Commission should have focus on the protection of the data of customers in the review of the *Google/*

---

[75] Hustinx (2013).

[76] Almunia (2012).

[77] Harbour (2014), pp. 225–234.

[78] Harbour (2014), pp. 225–234.

DoubleClick merger[79] for the creation of a massive amount of data on consumer behaviour. If the European Commission failed to look at data protection in that case, it later corrected the position in the review of the *TomTom/TeleAtlas* case[80] where data protection became part of the competitive analysis.

Under these precursory stances data protection is compared to a form of product degradation that could induce consumers to not deal with companies that cannot guarantee the respect of their confidential information and switch to more respectful competitors.[81]

However, what makes the financial information sector different is that credit bureaus cannot be punished by consumers because there is no privity of contract. In this case, data protection cannot become one of the non-economic dimensions that may influence consumer decision-making. Consumer choice is not at risk for consumers having no choice in the first place. If they want access to personal finance they must accept the processing and exchange of their data pooled via third-party providers.

Therefore, if conceptually there is an understanding that personal data protection may feature in the competition law analysis, what may be reductive is the exclusive focus on consumer choice as the test.

5.6.2 Personal Data Protection as Consumer Interest

Arguably, it is the position of the consumer as data subject and his/her interest in the information pertaining to him/her that needs to be revisited and find its definition in the information market.

The sector of financial information exchanges exemplifies that privity of contract may constitute an insurmountable barrier in any competition analysis if the values behind data protection themselves are not given independent non-price dimension position. Consumer profiling, economic sorting, classification and discrimination become part of the traded or tradable good and they require a definition in the marketplace beyond consumer choice.

Another possible dimension of the interplay between the two areas of law is the one that conceives personal data as a matter of competition if customers were prevented from switching from a company to another because they cannot carry their data along with them.[82]

---

[79] *Google/DoubleClick*, Case No. COMP/M.4731, available at http://ec.europa.eu/competition/mergers/cases/decisions/m4731_20080311_20682_en.pdf.

[80] *TomTom/TeleAtlas*, Case No COMP/M.4854, available at http://ec.europa.eu/competition/mergers/cases/decisions/m4854_20080514_20682_en.pdf.

[81] Harbour (2014), pp. 225–234; Hustinx (2013), Coates (2011).

[82] Hustinx (2013).

The Proposed Regulation contains in its provision an important novelty addressing data portability, that means that a consumer could be able to move or take with him/her the personal data easily and at no extra cost. The explanatory memorandum clearly explains it:

> Article 18 introduces the data subject's right to data portability, i.e. to transfer data from one electronic processing system to and into another, without being prevented from doing so by the controller. As a precondition and in order to further improve access of individuals to their personal data, it provides the right to obtain from the controller those data in a structured and commonly used electronic format.[83]

Such a provision may have the potential to challenge the business model of a third-party agency in the information exchange among competitors discussed so far. If and to the extent that consumers will be able to take with them their financial data from a financial institution to another, it remains to be seen what role credit bureaus may play in an unnecessary duplication of information. This is too early to determine and it should be left for further analysis upon the evolution of events.

But then again, if the relationship between data protection and competition is sensibly seen as a possible concern or impediment for the switching of consumers to a competitor, by the same token it is reasonable to argue for the opposite.

As briefly mentioned above in this work, personal data may be a barrier to switching in all those circumstances where the information is not seen positively by the competitor. If companies are influenced by the personal data generated by the relationship with its competitors, it will become biased towards the consumer. Until the moment when companies make their decision based on the decisions taken by others or as a result of the experience of others without developing their independent intelligence and strategies, information will remain a double-edged sword. This would be regardless of the existence of an intermediary agency or under a new right of data portability.

---

[83] Explanatory Memorandum, Proposal for a Regulation of the European Parliament and of the Council on the Protection of Individuals with regard to the Processing of Personal Data and on the Free Movement of Such Data (General Data Protection Regulation) COM/2012/011 final—2012/ 0011 (COD). Article 18 Right to data portability:

1. The data subject shall have the right, where personal data are processed by electronic means and in a structured and commonly used format, to obtain from the controller a copy of data undergoing processing in an electronic and structured format which is commonly used and allows for further use by the data subject.
2. Where the data subject has provided the personal data and the processing is based on consent or on a contract, the data subject shall have the right to transmit those personal data and any other information provided by the data subject and retained by an automated processing system, into another one, in an electronic format which is commonly used, without hindrance from the controller from whom the personal data are withdrawn.
3. The Commission may specify the electronic format referred to in paragraph 1 and the technical standards, modalities and procedures for the transmission of personal data pursuant to paragraph 2. Those implementing acts shall be adopted in accordance with the examination procedure referred to in Article 87(2).

5.6.3 Personal Data as a Commodity and Competition

The section above has shown how and why personal data protection is a fundamental right. At the same time, it is clear that personal information is a tradable or alienable commodity, which raises the issue to what extent there may be a market for fundamental rights. Under human rights theory, these rights are usually inalienable and none is tradable, but someone may freely choose to exercise his/her specific right or not. Therefore, if it is beyond doubt that there exist a reference market for personal data, the question arises as to how this would be compatible with the concept and values behind data protection that is felt so key for European societies to elevate its protection at the highest levels of EU legislation and as a fundamental right.

Chantal Mak interestingly points out how legal scholarship has long being divided over the real meaning of fundamental right and what it truly encapsulates. The author also demonstrates that the understanding of the meaning of 'fundamentality' differs from country to country. However, among the many differences, a basic common feature of the understanding of what accounts for a fundamental rights is the expression of a legal principle recognised as 'constitutional' which concerns human dignity and personal freedom.[84]

In theory, thus, the idea of tradable or alienable fundamental rights may look an oxymoron.

Generally, not many such other market examples exist. Some may think as the right to water of other natural resources as possible illustrations of other human rights containing a tradable element. Indeed, these are usually regulated markets also classified as Services of General Economic Interest (SGEI) services, which the public authorities classify as being of general interest and subject to specific public service obligations and regulated by a specific legislative framework. But personal data are not classified or treated as a SGEI service.

True, it would be a violation that breaches a fundamental right, therefore before engaging in any evaluation one should give proof of such an occurrence. Trading in data that are lawfully processed cannot be accounted as a violation of a fundamental right. But regardless of any compliance analysis, the uncontested issue is that when consumers deal with businesses, especially if these are financial institutions and the contract at stake is the provision of personal finance, there is a significant imbalance between the parties that leaves consumers with little or no alternative to give away their data and further dissemination if they want to have a chance.

The difficulty is that personal data in themselves have become a commodity. They make the market product. It is what is done later with the data that may be at odds with fundamental rights. For example, credit bureaus do not sell profiles or blacklists. They pass on the information as a decision-making tool for the lenders.

---

[84] Mak (2008).

They are the financial institutions that eventually derive consequences from the reading or interpretation of the information so obtained.

But at the same time economic sorting, discrimination, classifications, and conforming of economic behaviours originate and take shape from such personal data. The use that is made of the information via the exchange is known to information providers—actually they do engage in such business with the precise intention that data will be used for those purposes.

5.6.4 Data Protection as a Non-Economic Interest of Competition

In the end the discussion reverts to the recurring theme of this work, which is about the goals of competition law. Whether its scope of protection remains controversial, most competition lawyers and economists take the resilient stance that its rules are designed to protect economic interests and that other non-economic interests, as much important as they may be, should be left to the protection of other means or laws, in this instance data protection.

Equally, it has been noted how the judiciary has taken the same position, deferring to data protection law any assessment and carrying on a pure economic analysis, albeit biased by assumptions.

If this remains the reading of competition law, what in the end may be the real intersection for both competition law and data protection is that of concentration of a tradable commodity foreclosing competition under the shield of data protection. Data protection, if applied separately, may be used in the same fashion as a proprietary right such as intellectual property with the undesirable result of favouring the concentration of economic power regardless of abuses.

However, when personal data and fundamental rights more generally are involved, the effects on society would be excessive, ultimately posing a threat to constitutional values such as dignity and liberty, hence democracy.

When personal data are involved, a separate application of the two fields of law may also take to abnormal situations of legality where data are processed legitimately, competition rules are respected, but the end result is a concentration of personal information in a dominant company which will become the holder of a power beyond the commercial world.

To the extent that it is accepted that information is power and its use may determine, drive or influence not only the economic but also on the social life of consumers, then further thoughts should be given to the role of integrity of the legal system as a whole rather than the practical implications of the rules taken separately and in parallel.

This suggests an expansive view of competition law as a set of rules able to limit the creation of concentration of power by the industry beyond a pure economic calculation, capable of bringing data protection and its values within its ambit.

The ongoing argument, thus, is that competition law cannot be so distortive to favour economic outcomes that create abnormal situations elsewhere that may possibly be outlawed at a later stage by other laws or means.

Probably, the existence of a reference market for personal data and the underneath fundamental right element that accompanies them could finally present competition law with such a test. The association of the idea of a market interfering with fundamental rights may become the new frontier and ultimate challenge for the goals of competition law which could not remain anchored exclusively to neo-liberal economic analysis.

The final wider thought and frustration that remain in place is that the above conundrum—and ensuing concerns—may not exist if financial information were treated as an untradeable public good under the control of a public institution pursuing well-defined policy objectives in the public interest and under the rule of law.

5.7 Concluding Remarks

The consumer interest and the consumer detriment are key concepts that feature in competition law and its enforcement. Traditionally, their assessment has been dominated by economic analysis to enhance the consumer welfare. This view has also contributed to determine the concept of who is the consumer under competition law.

In the case at study, the consumer of the European competition authorities is not only a rational and vigilant consumer who maximises his/her own utility and who conforms his/her behaviour in accordance with the '*dicta*' of the financial services industry, but he/she is also one who is well placed in society and does not experience problems regardless of their nature. He/she is a consumer who is known to the financial industry for having developed a 'financial *curriculum vitae*' and for existing in a database.

This view of the consumer contradicts other areas of the law, *in primis* the image of the consumer under consumer protection law, as well as the new emerging concepts which encompass vulnerability and which inform consumer protection legislation.

All in all, therefore, competition law enforcement undertakes an unsatisfactory assessment which undermines the integrity of the legal system. Also, it biases the concept of 'interest' or 'detriment' of consumers.

The economic analysis and assessment of the consumer welfare remains important and may coexist with other interests, but it is argued that it cannot be exclusive and that 'all consumers generally' cannot be identified with those of the competition authorities in the cases and guidelines provided so far.

In addition, this work endorses that emerging literature which views the consumer interest under competition law as embracing also other non-economic interests.

But the other argument which it develops is that fundamental rights should be added into the equation. The case study of data protection and the information market provide an illustration that fundamental rights may become an important component of the assessment of the interest or detriment of consumers, who should be valued not only as economic agents but also as members of society.

Even if other areas of law are predisposed to grant protection to such values instead of competition law, there are instances where alone they cannot take a holistic perspective and offer adequate or just solutions. If the legal system operates with separate boxes for each area of law delegating possible issues to other boxes but nevertheless granting a decision, the integrity of the system as a whole may be compromised and it may take to abnormal situations. The argument is that the study of the exchange of information among competitors provides one of such examples.

References

Adler M and Wozniak E (1980) The origins and consequences of default—an examination of the impact of diligence. Research report n. 6, Scottish Law Commission

Albors-Llorens A (2006) Consumer law, competition law and the europeanization of private law. In: Cafaggi F (ed) The institutional framework of European private law. Oxford University Press, Oxford, p 245–270

Almunia J (2012) Competition and personal data protection. Privacy platform event: competition and privacy in markets of data, Brussels, 26 November 2012

Amato G (1997) Antitrust and the bounds of power: the dilemma of liberal democracy in the history of the market. Hart Publishing, Oxford

Andriychuk O (2009) Can we protect competition without protecting consumers? Compet Law Rev 6(1) 77–87

Balmer N, Pleasence P, Buck A, Walker H (2006) Worried sick: the experience of debt problems and their relationship with health, illness and disability. Soc Policy Soc 5(1):39–51

Banisar D, Davies S (1999) Global trends in privacy protection: an international survey of privacy, data protection, and surveillance laws and developments. John Marshall J Comput Inf Law 18:1–111

Becker GS (1976) The economic approach to human behavior. The University of Chicago Press, Chicago

Benöhr I, Micklitz HM (2010) Consumer protection and human rights. In: Howells G, Ramsay I, Wilhelmsson T, Kraft D (eds) Handbook of research on international consumer law. Edward Elgar, Cheltenham, pp 19–47

Berthoud R, Kempson E (1992) Credit and debt: the PSI report, PSI

Bishop S, Walker M (1999) The economics of EC competition law. Sweet and Maxwell, London

Bloustein EJ (1964) Privacy as an aspect of human dignity: an answer to dean prosser. N Y Univ Law Rev 39:962–1007

Bork RH (1993) The antitrust paradox. Free Press, New York

Buttigieg E (2009) Competition law: safeguarding the consumer interest. A comparative analysis of US Antitrust Law and EC Competition Law. Kluwer Law International, The Netherlands

Camerer C, Issacharoff S, Loewenstein G, O'Donoghue T, Rabin M (2003) Regulation for conservatives: behavioral economics and the case for asymmetric paternalism. Univ PA Law Rev 151:1211–1254

Caplovitz D (1963) The poor pay more: consumer practices of low income families. Free Press, New York

Cartwright P (2011) "The vulnerable consumer of financial services: law, policy and regulation", financial services research forum. University of Nottingham, Nottingham

Cartwright P (2010) Conceptualising and understanding fairness: lessons from and for financial services. In: Kenny M, Devenney J, Fox O'Mahony L (eds) Unconscionability in European private financial transactions: protecting the vulnerable. Cambridge University Press, Cambridge, pp 205–226

Coates K (2011) Competition law and regulation of technology markets. Oxford University Press, Oxford

Cseres KJ (2007) The controversies of the consumer welfare standard. Compet Law Rev 3(2):121–173

Davis SG (1997) Re-engineering the right to privacy: how privacy has been transformed from a right to a commodity. In: Agre PE, Rotenberg M (eds) Technology and privacy: the new landscape. The MIT Press, Cambridge, pp 143–165

De Hert P, Gutwirth S (2009) Data protection in the case law of Strasbourg and Luxembourg: constitutionalisation in action. In: Gutwirth S et al (eds) Reinventing data protection? Springer, Heidelberg, pp 3–44

de Vries SA (2013) Balancing fundamental rights with economic freedoms according to the European court of justice. Utrecht Law Rev 9(1):169–192

DeCew J (1997) In pursuit of privacy: law, ethics, and the rise of technology. Cornell University Press, Ithaca

Diamond P, Vartiainen H (eds) (2007) Introduction to behavioural economics and its applications. Princeton University Press, Princeton

Dine J, Fagan A (eds) (2006) Human rights and capitalism. Edward Elgar, Cheltenham

Dominy N, Kempson E (2003) Can't pay or won't pay? a review of creditor and debtor approaches to the non-payment of bills, DCA

Electronic Privacy Information Center and Privacy International (2002) Privacy and human rights 2002—an international survey of privacy laws and developments, Washington DC, London

Elliott A (2005) Not waving but drowning: over-indebtedness by misjudgement, CSFI

European Foundation for Financial Inclusion (2013) Financial inclusion and new means of payment, Brussels, May 2013

Evans P (2012) The consumer and competition policy: welfare, interest and engagement. In: Ezrachi A (ed) Research handbook on international competition law. Edward Elgar, Cheltenham, pp 545–564

Ferretti F (2007/2008) Consumer credit information and the abuse of individual rights in the EC: evidence from a legal compliance analysis. The need for a new European legal and institutional framework. Eur Consum Law J/Revue Européenne de Droit de la Consommation 1:87–130

Fried C (1970) An anatomy of values. Harvard University Press, Cambridge

Gavison R (1980) Privacy and the limits of the law. Yale Law J 89:421–471

Gerstein R (1978) Intimacy and privacy. Ethics 89:76–81

Hansen J, Kysar D (1999) Taking behaviouralism seriously: the problem of market manipulation. N Y Univ Law Rev 74:630–749

Haracoglou I (2007) Competition law, consumer policy and the retail sector: the systems' relation and the effects of a strengthened consumer protection policy on competition law. Compet Law Rev 3(2):175–208

Harbour PJ (2014) The transatlantic perspective: data protection and competition law. In: Hijmans H, Kranenborg H (eds) Data protection anno 2014: how to restore trust? Intersentia, Cambridge, pp 225–234

Harvey D (2005) A brief history of neoliberalism. Oxford University Press, Oxford

Heisenberg D (2005) Negotiating privacy. Lynne Rienner, London

Hoermann G (ed) (1986) Consumer credit and consumer insolvency: perspectives for legal policy from Europe and the USA, ZERP

Howells G, Weatherill S (2005) Consumer Protection Law. Ashgate, Aldershot

Hustinx P (2013) Data protection law in the context of competition law investigations. Seminar covington & burling LLP, Brussels, 13 June 2013

Inness J (1992) Privacy, intimacy, and isolation. Oxford University Press, Oxford

Jay R, Hamilton A (2003) Data protection—law and practice. Thomson Sweet & Maxwell, London

Jolls C, Sustain CR, Thaler R (1998) A behavioral approach to law and economics. Stanford Law Rev 50:1471–1550

Kang J, Bunter B (2004) Privacy in Atlantis. Harvard J Law Technol 18:230–267

Kenyon AT, Richardson M (2006) New dimensions in privacy: communications technologies, media practices and law. In: Kenyon AT, Richardson M (eds) New dimensions in privacy law. Cambridge University Press, Cambridge, pp 1–10

Lavrijssen S (2010) What role for national competition authorities in protecting non-competition interests after Lisbon? Eur Law Rev 35(5):636–659

London Economics (2010) Study on the economic benefits of privacy enhancing technologies—Final report to the European Commission DG Justice, Freedom, and Security (July 2010). http://ec.europa.eu/justice/policies/privacy/docs/studies/final_report_pets_16_07_10_en.pdf

MacCulloch A (2010) The consumer and competition law. In: Howells G, Ramsay I, Wilhelmsson T, Kraft D (eds) Handbook of research on international consumer law. Cheltenham, Edward Elgar, pp 77–106

MacDonald DA (2000) Myths in the privacy debate. In: CEI Staff (ed) The future of financial privacy. Competitive Enterprise Institute, Washington, DC, pp 54–75

Mak C (2008) Fundamental rights in European contract law—a comparison of the impact of fundamental rights on contractual relationships in Germany, the Netherlands, Italy and England. The Netherlands, Kluwer Law International

Mayer-Schonberger V (1997) Generational development of data protection in Europe. In: Agre PE, Rotenberg M (eds) Technology and privacy: the new landscape. The MIT Press, Cambridge, pp 219–241

Micklitz HW (ed) (2011a) The many concepts of social justice in European private law. Edward Elgar, Cheltenham

Micklitz HW (2013) Access to and exclusion from financial markets after the global financial crisis. In: Wilson T (ed) International responses to issues of credit and over-indebtedness in the wake of the crisis. Ashgate, Aldershot, pp 18–47

Micklitz HW (2011) Social justice and access justice in private law. In: Micklitz HW (ed) The many faces of social justice in private law. Edward Elgar, Cheltenham, pp 3–60

Micklitz HW (2006) The general clause of unfair practices. In: Howells G, Micklitz HW, Wilhelmsson T (eds) European fair trading law: the unfair commercial practices directive. Ashgate, Aldershot, pp 83–121

Monti G (2007) EC competition law. Cambridge University Press, Cambridge

Monti G (2002) Article 81 EC and public policy. Common Mark Law Rev 39:1057–1099

Moore A (1998) Intangible property: privacy, power, and information control. Am Philos Q 35:365–378

O'Donoghue R, Padilla J (2013) The law and economics of Article 102 TFEU. Hart Publishing, Oxford

Odudu O (2010) The wider concerns of competition law. Oxford J Legal Stud 30(3):599–613

Osovsky A (2013) The misconception of the consumer as a homo economicus: a behavioral-economic approach to consumer protection in the credit-reporting system. Suffolk Univ Law Rev 46(3):881–933

Parent W (1983) Privacy, morality and the law. Philos Public Aff 12:269–288

Parret L (2009–2010) Do we (still) know what we are protecting. TILEC discussion paper, pp 1–48

Paul J, Miller F, Paul E (eds) (2000) The right of privacy. Cambridge University Press, Cambridge

Pennock J, Chapman J (eds) (1971) Privacy, NOMOS XIII. Atherton Press, New York

Petit N, Neyrinck N (2010) A review of the competition law implications of the treaty on the functioning of the European union. Compet Policy Int 2:1–14

Rachels J (1975) Why privacy is important. Philos Public Aff 4:323–333

Ramsay I (2007) Consumer law and policy. Hart Publishing, Oxford

Ramsay I (2012) Consumer law and policy. Hart Publishing, Oxford

Regan P (1995) Legislating privacy. University of North Carolina Press, Chapel Hill

Reich N (1997) Competition law and the consumer. In: Gormley L (ed) Current and future perspectives on EC competition law. Kluwer, The Netherlands, pp 127–137

Riley A (2007) The EU reform treaty and the competition protocol: undermining EC competition law. CEPS policy brief. Centre for European Policy Studies, Brussels, 24 September 2007

Rodotà S (2009) Data protection as a fundamental right. In: Gutwirth S et al (eds) Reinventing data protection? Springer, Heidelberg, pp 77–82

Rosen J (2000) The unwanted gaze: the destruction of privacy in America. Vintage, New York

Rouvroy A, Poullet Y (2009) The right to informational self-determination and the value of self-development: reassessing the importance of privacy for democracy. In: Gutwirth S et al (eds) Reinventing data protection? Springer, Heidelberg, pp 45–76

Schober GM, Ghosh S, Bartow A, Hoofnagle C, Borzi-Panelists P (2002) Transcript: colloquium on privacy & security. Buffalo Law Review 50:703–754

Schoeman F (ed) (1984) Philosophical dimensions of privacy: an anthology. Cambridge University Press, Cambridge

Simitis S (1994–1995) From the market to the polis: the EU directive on the protection of personal data. Iowa Law Rev 80(3):445–469

Staten ME, Cate FH (2004) Does the fair credit reporting act promote accurate credit reporting? Working paper series BABC 04-14, joint center for housing studies, February 2004. Harvard University, Cambridge, MA

Stromholm S (1967) Right of privacy and rights of the personality. Stockholm, Norstedt

Stuyck J (2000) European consumer law after the treaty of Amsterdam: consumer policy in or beyond the internal market. Common Mark Law Rev 37:367–400

Townley C (2009) Article 81 EC and public policy. Hart Publishing, Oxford

Townley C (2011) Which goals count in Article 101 TFEU? Public policy and its discontents: the OFT's roundtable discussion on Article 101(3) of the Treaty on the Functioning of the European Union. Eur Compet Law Rev 32(9):441–448

Waddington L (2013) Vulnerable and confused: the protection of 'vulnerable' consumers under EU law. Eur Law Rev 38(6):757–782

Warren S, Brandeis L (1890) The right to privacy. Harvard Law Rev 4:193–220

Weatherill S (2007) Who is the 'Average Consumer'? In: Weatherill S, Bernitz U (eds) The regulation of unfair commercial practices under EC directive 2005/29. New rules and new techniques. Hart Publishing, Oxford, pp 115–138

Weitbrecht A (2008) From Freiburg to Chicago and beyond—the first 50 years of European competition law. Eur Compet Law Rev 29(2):81–88

Westin A (1967) Privacy and freedom. Atheneum, New York

Whish (2012) Competition law. Oxford University Press, Oxford

Wilhelmsson T (2004) The abuse of the 'Confident Consumer' as a justification for EC consumer law. J Consum Policy 27(3):317–337

Wilhelmsson T (2006) Misleading practices. In: Howells G, Micklitz HW, Wilhelmsson T (eds) European fair trading law: the unfair commercial practices directive. Ashgate, Aldershot, pp 123–165

Wilhelmsson T (2007) The paradox of the risk society and the fragmentation of consumer law. In: Ramsay I, Salloum J, Horrox N, Mowatt G (eds) Risk and choice in consumer society. Ant. N. Sakkoulas, Athens, pp 1–21

Williams T (2013) Continuity, not rupture: the persistence of neoliberalism in the internationalisation of consumer finance regulation. In: Wilson T (ed) International responses to issues of credit and over-indebtedness in the wake of the crisis. Ashgate, Aldershot, pp 15–46

Chapter 6
Conclusions: Policy and Legal Myopia?

This work examined the issue of the legitimacy or illegitimacy of information exchanges among competitors in the retail financial sector under EU competition law. In the market generally, information exchanges among competing undertakings are a controversial area which has generated legal debates and a degree of uncertainty as to their regulation and enforcement. In fact, on the one hand they may be a pro-competitive practice and a common feature of competitive markets because they are capable of generating efficiency gains; on the other hand, however, they may easily lead to collusion and restrictions of competition because competing undertakings become aware of the market strategies of their competitors.

In turn, competition authorities and the judiciary have not provided defined general or theoretical rules but they have offered guiding principles to be used on a case-by-case basis depending on the features of the market in which the exchange takes place, the economic context in which participants to the exchange operate, and the type of information exchanged.

Nonetheless, the bulk of case-law, guidelines by policy-makers, and academic debates have not resolved the difficulties of elaborating general and theoretical rules that provide the needed legal certainty. On the contrary, to the extent that some guidance has been offered so far, this is often oriented towards narrow aspects which are of limited scope and whose application may lead to abnormal or inconsistent outcomes.

This work revisited this grey area of competition policy and law enforcement taking as case study the exchange of consumer financial information in the context of the EU consumer financial market.

In particular, recognising the traditional economic objectives of competition law, it focused on the exchanges of personal financial data among competing lenders vis-à-vis market integration and the interest of consumers. In so doing, due

© The Author(s) 2014
F. Ferretti, *EU Competition Law, the Consumer Interest and Data Protection*,
SpringerBriefs in Law, DOI 10.1007/978-3-319-08906-5_6

attention has been given to the peculiarities of a market which is particularly sensitive for the potential detriment that it may pose to consumers and its close ties with their lives beyond economic agency. Indeed, the perspective taken by this study has been that if it is true that the traditional economic objectives of competition policy and law need to be accommodated, at the same time EU competition law enforcement must achieve market integration, but ultimately markets must work for consumers as human beings with all ensuing consequences.

Chapter 2 has shown that there are a variety of purposes or rationales for exchanging consumer financial information, some advanced by economic theory to address the market intelligence and profitability of the financial industry, while others to pursue defined public policy objectives under the rule of law. It has also shown that the information exchange may take different legal forms depending on the goals that it aims to reach.

The design of the information system, the type of information exchanged and the purpose, the level of detail of the information exchanged, its form, frequency and accuracy are important determinants in the assessment of the legitimacy or illegitimacy under traditional competition law. This has been investigated in Chap. 3, which also stressed the difficulties of elaborating general and theoretical rules to establish the legitimacy of exchanging information between competitors under competition law enforcement. The case-law and the literature point to an approach on a case-by-case basis which must include, in addition to the above, the economic context in which the participants to the exchange operate. Once it has been assessed whether or not such an exchange may have the potential to limit competition, in the affirmative case it should be investigated if such anti-competitive practice should be exempted for having a predominantly positive effect for consumers.

The *Asnef* case is the precedent setting the benchmark in the financial retail sector. It provides a clarification of the conditions in which financial institutions may operate. At the same time, it delegates national courts to determine whether the relevant markets are not concentrated, the system does not allow for the identification of lenders, and the conditions of access to the system are not discriminatory in law or in fact, which as said results in a case-by-case determination.

Equally, the *2011 Guidelines* incorporate a new section on the issue and are meant to provide legal clarity to market players, incorporating and consolidating the case-law of the CJEU, including *Asnef*.

However, when it comes to its substance the position taken by the competent European competition authorities may be criticised on a number of key points. The devil is in the details, as a proverb use to say. But when the details become so important to influence and guide the decisions towards a given outcome which is arguably contentious or unjust, they cannot be considered irrelevant niceties.

This work has recognised the virtues of the case-law and the official guidelines as far as the non-discrimination and the pro-competitive entry of foreign lenders in the national markets of the Member States are concerned.

At the same time, however, it is critical on a number of different grounds, starting from being limited to the sharing of negative financial data but leaving full uncertainty over positive and other data, to reliance on economic assumptions provided by the credit industry that are questionable and need demonstration, as well as juridical assumptions which blur or confuse policy objectives and institutions such as public credit bureaus with commercial entities doing business for their own profit and offering a service for the profitability of their members.

Most and foremost, however, it censures the jurisprudence of the CJEU and the official guidelines for failure to take a broader view of EU market integration and what may be needed to achieve it.

The European judiciary and the European Commission have focused on competitive markets for the financial services industry. Instead, the main culprit may be identified in the failure to identify and include a relevant market for information which has the potential to hinder the EU free movement rights.

Also, an analysis of the consumer information market point to monopolistic or oligopolistic situations which would require careful investigations, with far-reaching implications for the interoperability of national systems and EU integration not only in the information market but also in the retail finance market which it serves.

Overall, the limit of the competition authorities so far has been to concentrate exclusively on the assessment of the horizontal competition among financial institutions neglecting the information providers, vertical integrations, the information market as relevant market, and national monopolies and concentrations.

Arguably, these other dimensions of competition law itself need attention. Private commercial credit bureaus, as natural monopolies, offer a dimension to problems of information monopoly which is broader from that taken by the European competition authorities. This ranges from vertical relations between the credit bureaus themselves and their client members, as well as horizontal competition among the credit bureaus themselves which, in turn, lead to recognised concentration issues.

The problem is that the case law and the guidelines of the European competition authorities offer a legitimatisation at the level of competition among lenders but in so doing they establish a 'legitimised' concentration and information monopoly of commercial entities at a different level, raising far-reaching questions of how much power is society ready to concede in the hands of few companies and the kind of society where Europeans want to live in.

This latter consideration leads to the final, but certainly not less important, criticism of the stance taken by the European competition authorities. This has to do with the interpretation of the CJEU of the fair share of the benefit for consumers, or the consumer interest. Restating the assumptions upon which data sharing is based, and assigning to the credit bureau industry social functions well beyond their remit, the Court first states that the benefit should be on all consumers in the relevant market and not on members of categories of consumers, then it specifies that such benefit is for those consumers whom interest rates would be higher if lenders did not share information, thus referring to members of a category of consumers. The latter are those who are already in the database and have a good credit history. However, it leaves out those who do not have a credit history as well as the vulnerable consumers, taking into account that the vulnerable consumers is not a static group of people but that any consumer may potentially become vulnerable at any given time. Regardless of this reflection, the interpretation of who are 'all consumers' for the calculation of the benefit bears important social concerns and issues of social inclusion, access, and justice.

This is the same reason why this work is also critical with the interpretation of what should be accounted as 'consumer benefit' under competition law in the area of consumer financial services. It is aware of the tendency to interpret it as a short-term economic gain. Likewise, it is conscious of the traditional economic goals of competition law and the prevailing support of the literature.

At the same time, however, it argues that economic sorting, classification, discrimination, and generally the conforming of behaviours dictated by few market players are vital issues for the kind of society where free citizens want to develop their personality and where they want to live in, and therefore they should be included in the calculus. The ultimate suggestion is that fundamental rights such as data protection should be introduced in the equation to protect long-term interests of society generally which will reflect on consumers as citizens.

In the end, the main argument goes back to the main theme behind this work, which is about the non-economic interests and goals of competition policy ad law.

Whether or not protected by other means or laws, non-economic goals should be part of competition law enforcement. In particular, fundamental rights should become an integral part of competition law analysis, as suggested by data protection law that—if applied separately—may lead to concentration of economic power regardless of specific abuses tackled under its provisions.

All in all, the main conclusion is that so far competition authorities in the EU appear to have been myopic and the exchange of consumer financial data in the retail finance sector remains a conundrum with many more far-reaching elements to be looked at than those determined in the case law and contained in the *2011 Guidelines*.

Competition law should not remain in a legal box, as the other areas of law such as consumer law and data protection law. This would be at the expenses of the integrity of the legal system as a whole.

This suggests an expansive view of competition policy and law as a set of rules able to limit the concentration of power by undertakings beyond a pure economic calculus, but becoming able of bringing consumer protection, data protection, and their values within its ambit, bridging them in a market that works for consumers not only as economic agents but also as full members of society.

In the specific case at hand, solutions to correct some of the problems outlined in this work may not be as distant. For example, the importance of distinguishing the functions and role of public credit bureaus from those of private or commercial credit bureaus may stem some of the concerns and reconcile the latter with some needs of the financial services industry.

As far as strict competition is concerned, in particular, it has already been demonstrated empirically by others that public credit bureaus contribute to the intensification of competition under the rule of law and, as public authority, do not pose concentration problems and make the interest of society generally. Private or commercial credit bureaus, by contrast, do not show effects on market structure[1] and raise all the concerns discussed above in this work—on top of serving exclusively private interests of the financial industry.

In this specific instance, therefore, making use of a set of different arguments this work shares the conclusions that the EU Member States should avail themselves of public credit bureaus. This should allow better reconciliation or approximation of competition law with consumer policy and fundamental rights in the interest of society. To do so, EU policy makers need to consider the case for institutional re-thinking under a regulatory umbrella clearly shaping the use and design of databases to defined policy objectives in the public interest.

Reference

Giannetti C, Jentzsch N, Spagnolo G (2010) Information-sharing and cross-border entry in European banking. ECRI Research Report N. 11, Brussels

---

[1] Giannetti et al. (2010).